Drug workers:
what you need to know about...

DrugScope

1 | Mental health

Mental health problems are extremely common, with more than one in six people suffering from a diagnosable condition at any time. People who misuse drugs are even more likely to experience poor mental health, and people with mental health problems are more susceptible to becoming substance abusers.

Despite being so common widespread, mental illness is still surrounded by fear, prejudice and ignorance. People with mental health difficulties who also misuse drugs or alcohol face a double stigma, and are amongst the most vulnerable and marginalised individuals in society.

Mental health problems influence the way individuals think, feel and behave and this can significantly affect their relationships, work and quality of life. However, contrary to the stereotypes, most people are able to lead productive and fulfilling lives with the appropriate treatment and support. Many recover completely, even if others relapse from time to time.

Some people find medication helpful, but mental illness is more than just a medical condition and prescribed drugs generally alleviate symptoms rather than offering a cure. The causes of mental distress often lie in life experiences and the patterns of thinking, feeling and behaviour that individuals develop as a result. Many people find that by exploring non-medical approaches to treatment and changing the way they live, they can make a big improvement to their mental health.

This chapter provides basic information on mental disorders and their treatment, as well as looking at the problem of dual diagnosis, or co-morbidity – where a person has both a severe mental health illness and a substance misuse problem. The chapter also covers mental health services and practice pointers on what to do when you have concerns about a service user's mental health.

Common mental health problems

Neurosis is the most common form of mental distress and refers to normal feelings of anxiety, fear or low mood that become seriously out of proportion. Neuroses vary in severity from mild and transient to severe and disabling.

Depression

Depression describes a range of moods from the low spirits we all experience from time to time to a severe problem that interferes with everyday life. A person who is 'clinically depressed' may experience:

1

- sadness and low mood

- loss of interest and pleasure

- loss of concentration and motivation

- feelings of guilt and worthlessness

- disturbed sleep patterns, e.g. difficulties sleeping and waking very early

- reduced or increased appetite and weight

- anxiety, agitation and irritability

- feelings that life is not worth living

- suicidal feelings or self-harm actions.

Depression usually lifts spontaneously after a period of several months, however it can also be chronic and disabling. A severely depressed person may be unable to cope with ordinary, everyday tasks like housework and looking after themselves, and may be at risk of suicide.

Depression may be triggered by events or experiences such as the death of someone close, a major life change (such as moving house or changing jobs) or simply passing from one phase of life into another, as when someone reaches retirement or children leave home. People coping with difficult circumstances such as homelessness and poverty are also vulnerable to depression. Less commonly, depression may have no apparent trigger. Some experts consider depression to be a form of unfinished mourning, and experiences that trigger it can often be seen as a loss of some kind.

However, it is not just the negative experience that causes the depression, but how the person deals with it. If the feelings provoked are not expressed or explored at the time, they can fester and contribute towards depression. Poor diet, lack of physical fitness, and illnesses such as flu can all leave someone feeling depressed. Frequent use of some recreational drugs can also play a part.

Treatment for depression

Talking treatments (counselling, psychotherapy and cognitive behaviour therapy) can be helpful for people suffering from depression. Cognitive behaviour therapy (CBT) may be particularly effective because it may help the person to tackle the negative patterns of thinking that feed the depression. Psychiatrists and GPs often prescribe antidepressants which may alleviate the symptoms, enabling the sufferer to take action to tackle the depression. Some people find complementary therapies, including acupuncture, massage and homeopathy, helpful. Physical exercise and dietary changes such as taking omega-3 oil supplements have also been shown to be beneficial.

Where depression is very severe and a person is suicidal, hospital admission may be appropriate to enable the person to be looked after and the effects of different treatments to be monitored.

Anxiety

Anxiety is a universal human emotion which is only regarded as a mental health problem when it is chronic and persistent.

- **Generalised anxiety** is free-floating anxiety which is with a person most of the time, rather than being triggered by a specific external stimulus.

- **Phobias** are a specific type of anxiety associated with a particular trigger and include agoraphobia (fear of open spaces) and social phobia (fear of meeting people).

- **Panic attacks** are associated with phobias and other anxiety states, but may also be experienced by people who have not previously suffered from anxiety. The person has a sudden and intense sensation of fear and impending doom, which is accompanied by breathlessness or hyperventilation, tremor, palpitations, giddiness and sweating.

- **Obsessive-compulsive disorder** involves distressing repetitive thoughts which the person knows their own (unlike hallucinations) but cannot ignore, and ritual actions which a person feels compelled to repeat to relieve anxiety or temporarily stop obsessional thoughts. For example, the sufferer may have an obsessional thought that their hands are dirty and repeatedly wash them over and over again.

Treatment for anxiety disorders

Although doctors can prescribe tranquillisers to relieve anxiety, these are only a short-term measure because of the problems of dependency and withdrawal which can leave a sufferer feeling worse than before they began taking them. Talking treatments such as CBT can help the sufferer to understand and deal with the causes of their anxiety and learn how to cope.

Self-help

Breathing and relaxation techniques, yoga and meditation can be effective in aiding the sufferer to manage their symptoms and get on with their lives. Physical exercise discharges the adrenaline and other stress hormones produced by anxiety and so helps to relieve tension and anxiety, and lift mood.

Sufferers should avoid stimulants such as tobacco and caffeine, which can cause anxiety. Complementary therapies such as massage, acupuncture and reflexology may also be helpful.

Post-traumatic stress disorder (PTSD)

Post-traumatic stress disorder is defined as the development of characteristic symptoms from psychologically distressing experiences which are outside the range of normal experience, such as torture, rape, destruction of a person's home or community, harm or threat of harm to family and friends, etc. Survivors of childhood abuse or domestic violence may also suffer from PTSD. Common symptoms include flashbacks and nightmares, avoidance of things associated with the trauma which may trigger chronic anxiety, panic, sleep disturbance and poor concentration. These are essentially normal responses to abnormal events, but survivors sometimes develop severe and long-term mental health problems.

Treatment

Talking treatment sessions with a clinical psychologist seem to be the most effective treatment for PTSD, although sufferers may also benefit from taking antidepressants.

Psychosis

Psychosis is a more serious form of mental illness and involves a distortion of a person's perception of reality, often accompanied by delusions or hallucinations. Anyone can have a transient psychotic episode, which may be triggered by bereavement, a traumatic experience or extreme stress. Recurrent and prolonged episodes are usually regarded as severe mental illness.

Schizophrenia

Schizophrenia is a diagnosis given to people who have episodes of severely disrupted beliefs and perceptions. The illness affects a person's thinking, mood and behaviour. Sufferers may lose touch with reality and see, hear, smell or feel things which are not there (hallucinate) and react in unusual ways to these hallucinations. They may also believe they are being controlled by outside forces. People often experience tiredness and loss of concentration and a lack of energy and motivation. These symptoms can make it impossible for sufferers to cope with everyday tasks.

Schizophrenia most commonly starts during the late teens or early 20s. Around 1 in 100 people experience a schizophrenic episode at some time during their life. Around a quarter recover fully while most others are able to lead a satisfactory life, albeit with some adjustments.

Treatment

Schizophrenic symptoms can be controlled using antipsychotic medication (also known as major tranquillisers or neuroleptics) which do not cure the illness but in many people reduce the psychotic symptoms and enable them to lead normal lives. However, antipsychotic medication can cause a range of unpleasant side effects, including involuntary movement, tremor, reduced sexual desire and restlessness, and there is a risk of permanent damage to the central nervous system, particularly in high doses. New antipsychotic drugs (known as atypicals) have generally reduced side effects.

Despite having been prescribed for many years there is still an element of controversy surrounding the prescription of antipsychotics, in particular for people experiencing their first psychotic episode for whom there is evidence that prescribing drugs may increase their chances of becoming ill in the long term. But there is also evidence that people who receive early treatment for their first psychotic episode are more likely to get on with their lives normally.

Some psychological therapies such as cognitive behaviour therapy can be helpful in reducing self-harming behaviour and delusional beliefs. There is also growing interest in complementary therapies, relaxation and other approaches which people use to manage their illness, usually in addition to antipsychotic medication.

Manic depression

Manic depression, also known as bipolar affective disorder, is a mood disorder characterised by extreme swings from euphoria to depression. During manic phases the person has excessive energy and little need for sleep. Their thinking and speech tend to speed up and their thoughts jump rapidly from one subject to another. Typically they have overblown ideas or delusions, a loss of inhibitions and inflated self-esteem. They may behave in a grandiose fashion, giving away possessions, spending a lot of money or leaving their job.

During a severe depressive episode a person experiences feelings of hopelessness and despair, lethargy, broken sleep, overwhelming negativity and difficulty carrying on with the activities of day-to-day life.

Some people with manic depression have long periods without experiencing problems and are able to hold down demanding jobs, but others are severely disabled by the disorder.

Treatment

Manic depression can often be effectively treated with mood stabilising medication (lithium). Talking treatments including CBT can also be helpful. People who are suffering from acute episodes may be admitted to hospital for assessment and treatment.

Personality disorders

The term personality disorder is often used by psychiatrists to describe someone who does not fit into any obvious diagnostic category, but has difficulty coping with life and whose behaviour persistently causes distress to themselves or others. Common problems include having difficulty sustaining relationships and interpreting social cues. Diagnoses include:

- borderline personality disorder

- antisocial personality disorder

- dependent personality disorder

- paranoid personality disorder.

Personality disorders can be seen as extreme examples of tendencies that everybody shares. Negative personality traits and extremes of behaviour are often regarded as quite excusable and unremarkable in gifted, famous or socially dominant individuals.

Diagnosing personality disorders is controversial because the problems are seen by many psychiatrists as too deep seated to be treatable. The diagnosis is also open to error, especially since the label is frequently used to describe symptoms that do not fit into any other category. Often, the diagnoses are applied to people who are regarded as 'difficult' in some way. Many survivors of domestic violence or child abuse have been mistakenly diagnosed with a personality disorder because the post-traumatic symptoms they developed as a result are so persistent and wide ranging, and are misread as being part of their basic personality.

Borderline personality disorder

Psychiatrists may give the diagnosis borderline personality disorder where a person shows a number of the following signs:

- self-harm or attempted suicide

- avoidance of being alone

- difficulties with relationships, e.g. seeing someone as wonderful one minute and wholly bad the next

- shaky self-image

- moods of irritability, unhappiness or anxiety

- harmful and impulsive behaviour such as drug or alcohol abuse, driving recklessly, bingeing on food, alcohol, shopping, etc

- feelings of terrible emptiness

- intense feelings of anger which may be inappropriate and difficult to control

- feelings of paranoia or unreality when under stress.

The disorder is often associated with traumatic experiences in childhood such as abuse or neglect and may also be linked with drug and alcohol misuse. Recent research suggests that people do get better as they get older and that after ten years as many as half of those with a borderline personality disorder no longer have symptoms severe enough to merit the diagnosis.

Antisocial personality disorder (APD)

Also known as 'psychopathy', this is the disorder most closely linked with adult criminal behaviour. Someone with APD is likely to ignore and ride roughshod over other people's rights. Although charming on the surface, they may be callous and self-serving underneath, and lack any empathy with other people.

They may not be able to hold down a job for any length of time or stay in a long-term relationship. They may behave impulsively, without considering the consequences, and this is often linked to criminal offences, particularly involving violence. Central to the problem is a complete lack of guilt about their behaviour.

There seems to be a higher rate of alcoholism and substance misuse among people with APD than in the rest of the population, and the effect of alcohol or drugs makes their behaviour even more extreme.

Treatment of personality disorders

Some psychiatrists regard personality disorders as untreatable because they are so deep-rooted and part of a person's basic personality. However, there is evidence that talking therapies, CBT and medication can reduce behavioural problems. Day-care programmes and alternative therapies may also be useful.

Dementia

Dementia is a disease of ageing, affecting 3% of those over 65 and 10–15% of people over 80. It involves a progressive decline in memory, thinking, problem-solving, concentration and perception. Dementia in people under 60 is rare and known as pre-senile dementia. There is no cure for dementia although some people find medication helpful.

Drugs and mental health problems

> Gary Jones began smoking cannabis heavily at the age of 16. Eighteen months later he was compulsorily admitted to hospital. His mother explains: 'We knew that something was going wrong, but we didn't know whether this was normal adolescent behaviour. We know now that he was using drugs to quell the voices in his head. He said that street drugs were far better than the ones he was getting from the doctor.'

Around a third of the people who use drug and alcohol services also have a severe mental health problem, although they may not have contact with mental health services. The proportion affected by more common mental health problems is much higher.

Dual diagnosis or **co-morbidity** are the terms used to describe people who misuse drugs or alcohol and who also have a severe mental health problem, such as schizophrenia or manic depression. The terms are also sometimes used to cover people who misuse drugs and have common mental health problems such as depression and anxiety.

Separating out symptoms caused by mental health problems and those linked to drink or drugs is notoriously difficult. The symptoms of schizophrenia or manic depression can be almost identical to those of someone who is intoxicated, suffering from amphetamine- or crack-induced psychosis, or withdrawing from drugs. In theory, people can fall into three categories:

- people whose mental health problems are directly caused by drugs or alcohol
- people using drugs which exacerbate mental health problems
- people using drugs to relieve mental health problems.

There is overlap between these categories, for example, where a drug-induced psychosis is masking real mental health problems. It is not uncommon for someone to suffer from more than one mental health problem, for example, a personality disorder and schizophrenia, and also to misuse drugs.

A period of three to six weeks abstaining from drugs is generally needed to help make a clear diagnosis, as drug-induced symptoms usually disappear over this time period. However, the person may be unwilling or unable to co-operate because they do not want to or cannot stop using drugs.

Drugs that can cause mental health problems

Stimulant drugs – cocaine, crack and amphetamines (speed)

Stimulant drugs can cause psychotic symptoms including hallucinations, paranoia and distressing thoughts. They can also cause unpleasant and distressing symptoms such as agitation and restlessness. Symptoms of drug-induced psychosis usually pass quite quickly after the person stops using the drug, although medication may still be required.

Cannabis

There is evidence that heavy cannabis use is linked with psychotic episodes. Generally, these lapse when the person stops using, but some psychiatrists believe that cannabis use can actually trigger schizophrenia in certain individuals who may have a genetic predisposition to the illness.

Alcohol

Heavy drinking can cause psychotic symptoms, particularly hallucinations and paranoia. It is also linked with low mood and physical problems when withdrawing.

Heroin and other opiates

Some heroin users describe themselves as being depressed, but this could be due to associated difficulties rather than the action of the drug itself.

Tranquillisers

People who take tranquillisers (Valium, 'benzos', etc) often develop a physical dependence and experience symptoms of anxiety if they stop using.

Drugs that can aggravate mental problems

Cannabis, LSD, stimulants, alcohol and **ecstasy** can all amplify the mood of the user. So if someone takes the drug when they are already feeling depressed, paranoid or anxious,

1

they may feel worse, depending on the environment and the quantity they use. Although these drugs can also lift a person's mood, on balance someone with a pre-existing mental health problem who uses them is likely to have their symptoms exacerbated.

Drugs that people use to relieve mental health problems

Some people with mental health problems may begin using combinations of street drugs and alcohol as an attempt at self-medication, believing that they will help relieve symptoms of distress or the unpleasant side effects of prescribed medication. Generally, rather than using a specific drug as self-medication, people are likely to use any drug to relieve distress with their choice of substance being determined mostly by availability and culture. Although people may experience temporary relief from unpleasant or disturbing symptoms, or the side effects of prescribed medication, there is little evidence that street drugs or alcohol are beneficial for mental health problems.

Downers (which include opiates, alcohol, cannabis and tranquillisers or 'benzos') are sedatives and slow down the central nervous system. They may, in the short term, reduce anxiety and give feelings of euphoria, and so may be attractive to people struggling to cope with distressing physical or mental symptoms. Over time, people using these drugs (with the exception of cannabis) become tolerant and so have to use more to get the same effect.

Uppers (which include amphetamines, cocaine and ecstasy) speed up the central nervous system, stimulating the mind and body. Users may experience feelings of well being, confidence, stamina and alertness. However, users can also develop psychological dependence on these drugs.

Assessment of people with co-morbidity

Recognising co-morbidity can be difficult because the signs and symptoms of mental illness and drug misuse or withdrawal can be identical. People with this combination of problems often have a lot of other difficulties in their lives. For example, they may have:

- a history of homelessness, attempted suicide and/or contact with the criminal justice system

- a history of relapse from psychiatric and substance abuse treatment

- a poor response to substance misuse treatment

- limited insight into the nature of their problems and lack understanding of the effects of substances, attributing them to mental illness or vice versa (hardly surprising, given that professionals often do this as well)

- memory and concentration difficulties, which are common with both mental illness and substance misuse.

People experiencing mental distress tend to find coping with interviews difficult. Corroborative information from relatives and other agencies is very useful in making an assessment.

Working with people with dual diagnosis

'There's a lack of access for people who lead chaotic lives. If you miss three appointments, you can't access services. It's about sorting out the basics first, like housing, so they're not on the streets and can begin treatment. Women turn up desperate for help but they're not able to get it.' Drug worker in Middlesbrough

- People with dual diagnosis are often seen as chaotic and difficult to treat, or even as 'hopeless cases'. But good contact with services often results in a good outcome.

- Initially, engaging the client may take time. Providing help with practical needs such as housing and benefits can ease pressures on the person and help in developing close contact – a first step to engaging them in treatment.

- People with dual diagnosis may have had many bad experiences of relapse and treatment which has been inappropriate or ineffective. They may lack motivation as a result and also because of their high level of mental distress. Using techniques of 'motivational interviewing' to strengthen a client's motivation and commitment to change can be effective.

- A non-confrontational and empathic approach generally works best in engaging highly vulnerable people.

- Medically orientated services are not always effective for people with complex problems that are not just psychiatric or psychological, and reflect the social stigma which people with dual diagnosis experience.

Services for people with dual diagnosis

'Lots of the people we work with find that drugs or alcohol give them some relief from their symptoms. We help them to look at reasons why they are using and to see what makes them feel better and worse. We often find people have to go

around a number of different services. People with crack psychosis are often told by mental health services that they have to give up the crack. They don't find that very helpful. Clinical outcomes tend to be better with one practitioner.' Worker in hostel for people with drug problems

Historically, people with dual diagnosis have received a raw deal from services, finding themselves shuttled between mental health and drug and alcohol treatment services, and frequently receiving inadequate or even no treatment at all. Drug users have often been excluded from psychiatric services because staff assume that the main problem is addiction and demand that people stop using drugs before they are assessed for treatment, which may be unrealistic. Drug workers may have little knowledge or understanding of mental illness.

Things are improving with much greater awareness of the need to co-ordinate mental health and drug and alcohol treatment services. There is no standardised treatment for dual diagnosis, but the current policy is that mental health services should provide care and treatment for people whose mental health problems are severe, with drug and alcohol services providing specialist support.

There are also a number of pilots providing integrated treatment for people with dual diagnosis, but integrated services are unlikely to be established in areas where there are relatively few people with co-morbidity. Increasingly, community mental health services employ substance abuse specialists and drug services have dual diagnosis specialist nurses working as part of the team.

What you should do if you are worried about a client's mental health

In most areas, the normal procedure for a drug worker who is worried about a person's mental health is to refer them to the community mental health team (CMHT) for assessment by a psychiatrist.

If the CMHT fails to diagnose a mental health problem and you are still worried, you may need to refer the client again. It could be that the CMHT sees the person on a good day and so does not pick up on the problems. An alternative option may be to arrange for the person to be assessed by a psychiatrist at a drug service.

Many drug services now employ specialist nurses trained in dual diagnosis who can carry out assessments. For less serious problems, such as anxiety or depression, it may be more appropriate to refer a patient to their GP or the local psychological service.

What if the person is suicidal or in crisis?

If you are worried that a person's state of mind is putting themselves or other people at risk, you should call the crisis team who have specialist assessors. They are the gatekeepers of mental health inpatient wards and have powers to section people. Stay with the person until the crisis team arrives.

What is 'sectioning'?

Sectioning is the procedure under the Mental Health Act 1983 (covering England and Wales) for compulsorily admitting to hospital a person who is suffering from a mental disorder and who needs to be detained for assessment for their own health or safety or for the protection of others.

- Usually, two doctors (one of whom must be specially approved) must agree that the person needs to be in hospital and an approved social worker decides whether or not to make an application.

- Exceptionally, the nominated nearest relative may make an application.

- In an urgent situation where there is no time to wait for another medical recommendation, a person may be admitted to hospital compulsorily, with only one medical recommendation. The second medical recommendation must be obtained within 72 hours.

There are plans to revise mental health legislation in England, Wales and Northern Ireland. Proposals include widening the category of people who can section someone (specialist nurses, for example, rather than only approved social workers) and, controversially, changing the provisions affecting compulsory treatment to include people with addiction.

Sectioning in Scotland

Compulsory detention and treatment powers in Scotland are contained in the Mental Health (Care and Treatment) Scotland Act 2003. This legislation provides for:

- **Emergency detention** This allows someone to be detained in hospital for up to 72 hours, where admission is required urgently to allow the person's condition to be assessed. It can only take place if recommended by a doctor, and wherever possible, the agreement of a mental health officer (a social worker specially trained in mental health) should also be obtained.

- **Short-term detention** This allows someone to be detained in hospital for up to 28 days. It can only take place when recommended by a psychiatrist and agreed by a mental health officer.

- **Compulsory treatment order (CTO)** This has to be approved by a tribunal, on application by a mental health officer. The application must include two medical recommendations and a plan of care detailing the care and treatment proposed for the patient. The patient, the patient's named person and the patient's primary carer are entitled to have any of their objections heard by the tribunal. The patient and the named person are entitled to free legal representation for the tribunal hearing.

- **Nurses' holding power** If a patient is in hospital receiving treatment on a voluntary basis and decides to leave the hospital, an appropriately qualified nurse can hold the patient for up to two hours to allow a doctor to come and assess the patient and decide whether detention in hospital is appropriate. The two-hour period can be extended by another hour once the doctor arrives.

- **Removal to a place of safety** If someone in a public place appears to have a mental disorder and be in need of care and treatment, the police can take that person to a place of safety. The individual can be kept there for up to 24 hours, to allow an assessment to be carried out about whether arrangements need to be made for the person's care and treatment.

For further information, see the briefing published by the Scottish Association for Mental Health at: www.samh.org.uk/newmentalhealthact/pdfs/mentalhealthactshortintro.pdf

Mental health services

Primary care

Local GP surgeries provide care for people experiencing problems such as depression or anxiety, and as well as prescribing medication may offer advice or counselling. They can also refer people whose problems are more severe to the local community mental health team, an outpatient psychiatry clinic or a psychology department, or for an assessment for community care services. All GPs study psychiatry as part of their general training and some have undertaken specialist training in the field. Few have specific training in dual diagnosis.

Community mental health teams (CMHTs)

CMHTs include community psychiatric nurses, social workers, clinical psychologists, occupational therapists, doctors and support workers. Most teams also now have a dual diagnosis specialist. Usually one member of the team will act as a key worker for each client. The key worker assesses people, monitors their mental health needs and ensures they receive the treatment, help and support they need to live as independently as possible.

Care Programme Approach

People with severe mental health problems (including people with dual diagnosis) should be subject to the Care Programme Approach. This involves a full systematic assessment covering mental and physical health, and also social need including housing and money. In addition, the assessment should include the participation of friends, relatives and other professionals or agencies working with the client. Once the client's needs are assessed, the key worker and client draw up a care plan specifying social, physical and/or psychological interventions, and in some cases support for the carer. Regular reviews should then take place to monitor the effectiveness of the plan and to adjust it accordingly.

Community care services

Social services and local voluntary organisations provide facilities in the community for people with mental health problems, for example day centres and drop-in centres which offer social activities, creative workshops, alternative therapies, keep fit classes, refreshments, advice and support with employment and welfare rights. They also provide residential facilities including care homes, hostels and supported housing (see Chapter 5: Housing).

Crisis intervention

Many areas provide crisis intervention teams to support people in the community without the need to admit them to hospital. This may include crisis beds in small community homes where the provision is much more informal than in hospital. Demand for community-based beds is high and it can be hard to find one for a client in crisis.

Hospital-based services

With the progressive closure of long-stay mental hospitals over the past 40 years, only a small minority of people with severe mental health problems now receive inpatient care. Most inpatient provision is for people who are acutely ill and who require nursing care

1

where the effects of treatment can be monitored. Stays of a few weeks are the norm while the person recovers. A minority of inpatient wards are locked or secure and are for people who are at risk of harming themselves or others who have been detained under mental health legislation.

Mental health trusts also run outpatient psychiatry clinics where patients meet a psychiatrist for assessment or review of their treatment.

Psychology

Mental health trusts provide psychological services based in community health centres or hospitals, offering a range of individual and group therapies including cognitive behavioural therapy. Practitioners include nurses and occupational therapists as well as clinical psychologists. Clients can be referred by a GP or psychiatrist, and sometimes can self-refer.

Services for young people (Child and Adolescent Mental Health Services)

Health trusts provide community-based Child and Adolescent Mental Health Services (CAMHS) for children and teenagers experiencing mental distress and those with severe behavioural problems. However, they may not be geared up for dealing with young people who are experiencing psychotic episodes, who may be referred to adult services.

Teenagers can be particularly vulnerable to using drugs as a means of dealing with unhappiness and other problems in their lives. Some areas have developed multidisciplinary teams to work with young people with co-morbidity. However, not all CAMHS teams have expertise in relation to youngsters who misuse drugs.

'Of the 400–500 young people aged between 14 and 18 referred to the local CAMHS team, around a quarter have significant substance misuse problems. 'There's a strong association between trauma and substance abuse – numbing your brain with anything you can get. Many of the young people I work with who have disciplinary problems and are using drugs – the so-called 'bad kids' – also have a lot of sadness in their lives. Some have suffered neglect or abuse, or post-traumatic stress disorder from war or conflict. They use drugs as a way of dealing with their problems. Many of these young people have multiple needs and a chaotic lifestyle. If you want to help them you have to go out to them.'
Psychiatrist working in south London

Useful organisations

Mind

Provides a helpline for people with mental health problems and their families/carers, and information about local services run by Mind.

Tel: 020 8519 2122

Website: www.mind.org.uk/information

Northern Ireland Association for Mental Health

Central Office
80 University Street
Belfast BT7 1HE

Tel: 028 9032 8474

Website: www.niamh.co.uk

Rethink

Provides support and runs local groups for people affected by severe mental illness.

Tel: 020 8547 3862

The Samaritans

Provides support and advice for people in crisis.

Tel: 0845 790 9090

Saneline

Offers help for people coping with mental illness and provides information about local services.

Tel: 0845 767 8000

The Scottish Association for Mental Health

Cumbrae House
15 Carlton Court
Glasgow G5 9JP

Tel: 0141 568 7000

Fax: 0141 568 7001

Email: enquire@samh.org.uk

Website: www.samh.org.uk

Young minds

Offers an advice line for parents, carers and professionals who are worried about a child or teenager's mental and emotional well-being.

Tel: 0800 018 2138 (not 24 hours)

References

Advisory Council on the Misuse of Drugs (2003) *Hidden Harm*, Home Office

Department Education and Skills *An Overview of Cross Government Guidance: Every Child Matters Change for Children*, 2005 available on line at www.everychildmatters.gov.uk

Scottish Executive (2002) *Getting Our Priorities Right: Good practice guidance for working with children and families affected by substance misuse*

2 Blood-borne viruses

This chapter contains key facts on the HIV and hepatitis viruses that pose a threat to the health of people who use drugs. It brings together information on:

- how each virus is spread

- the tests used to diagnose infection, and what they mean

- the likely health consequences for someone who is infected

- what can be done to prevent the spread of infection, including vaccination where available.

It is important to offer education and prevention advice on blood-borne viruses to all drug users and not only to those identified as injecting drug users. The following rationales suggest that education, advice and vaccination should be offered at the earliest possible opportunity.

- Oral drug users can progress to injecting.

- Injecting drug users have often been injecting for several years before they report their injecting behaviour to services.

- Initiation into injecting is a very high-risk time for transmission of these viruses, as the new injector is often reliant on others to help him/her inject and may be much less able to control the risk factors for infection. This experimental phase is likely to occur before they have discussed injecting drugs with a professional.

- For some of these viruses, sexual transmission is an important possible route of transmission.

- Individuals will take one to two months after completion of their course of vaccination to achieve maximum immunity.

- More research on the exact transmission routes of hepatitis C within the drug-using population are required and some studies show significantly high infection rates in drug users who give no history of injecting. The possible reasons for this are as yet unexplained.

Hepatitis

Hepatitis means inflammation of the liver. It is a disease most commonly caused by viral infection. It can also be caused by:

- drinking too much alcohol

- the side effects of some drugs and chemicals

- a rare autoimmune disease in which the body's immune system malfunctions and attacks the liver.

There are many different viruses that affect the liver and these are described by different initials: A, B, C, D, E and G. These viruses differ in how they are spread, the way they affect the liver and the consequences for health.

Hepatitis A, B and C are the three hepatitis viruses of concern for drug users in the UK.

Symptoms of hepatitis

Acute symptoms of hepatitis are similar no matter which type of hepatitis a person has. Many people do not get any acute symptoms and therefore will not know they are or have been infected. If symptoms do occur, individuals may experience any or all of the following:

- fever

- loss of appetite

- fatigue

- joint pain

- abdominal pain

- diarrhoea

- vomiting

- dark urine

- jaundice.

Very rarely, an acute (new) case of viral hepatitis can cause liver failure and require hospital admission. Of these acute cases requiring hospital admission, 1% may die without immediate liver transplant.

Hepatitis A only ever causes an acute illness. Both hepatitis B and C can cause either acute or chronic infection (still present after six months) and can have much more serious long-term health consequences.

Notification

Acute hepatitis is a notifiable disease in the UK. This means acute infection must be reported to the local Public Health Department either by the doctor requesting the test or by the laboratory carrying out the test.

Notification should provide the opportunity to identify close contacts of the infected individual and offer them appropriate testing and vaccination.

Hepatitis A

What is hepatitis A?

Hepatitis A is an acute illness caused by infection with the hepatitis A virus. The terms hep A or HAV can be used as abbreviations either for the disease or the virus itself. The majority of adults who become infected have symptoms which include jaundice within six weeks of being infected. They are most infectious two weeks before the onset of jaundice. The risk of transmitting the infection falls rapidly after jaundice has appeared.

How is it spread?

Hepatitis A virus is found in the faeces of infected persons. Hepatitis A is usually spread by the faeco-oral route, i.e. something being placed in the mouth which has been contaminated with the faeces of an infected person.

There have been several outbreaks of hepatitis A infection in injecting drug using (IDU) populations in the UK. IDUs may be at higher risk of hepatitis A infection due to poor living conditions often associated with homelessness. In these outbreaks, transmission is thought to be possible via three main routes:

- the faeco-oral route

- through contamination of drugs or injecting paraphernalia

- through needle sharing when the hepatitis A positive person is viraemic (carrying high levels of the virus in their bloodstream).

What happens when a person is infected?

Incubation period

There is an average period of four weeks (range two to six weeks) between the virus entering the body and the appearance of any symptoms.

Diagnosis

A blood test for HAV-specific immunoglobulin (**IgM**) will confirm the diagnosis and is usually present before the onset of symptoms.

Antibodies

After HAV infection, antibodies are developed which protect against re-infection.

Acute hepatitis A

Any of the acute symptoms of hepatitis may occur. There is no specific treatment for HAV but the person may need rest and support during any acute symptoms. Most people will begin to recover within a few months. Very occasionally, people who are elderly or have weak immune systems can become more seriously ill and require admission to hospital.

Hepatitis A is a notifiable infectious disease. The local Public Health Department will be involved in tracing close household contacts that may be at risk and will offer them immunoglobulin or vaccination to protect them from infection if this is necessary.

There is no chronic infection with HAV.

Key prevention issues

Good personal hygiene and careful hand washing are crucial in preventing the spread of infection. Vaccination should be encouraged for those whose lifestyle may place them at increased risk.

Vaccination

Vaccination against hepatitis A is recommended for all IDUs and people who are infected with HIV or HCV. It can be given singly or in a combined vaccine with hepatitis B. Funding of this, however, is organised at local health authority level and availability is variable. The Public Health Consultant in your area should be able to advise how and where vaccination is available.

Vaccine	*Schedule*
Single hepatitis A	2 doses 6–12 months apart The second dose may be delayed for up to 3 years
Combined hepatitis A & B (twinrix)	Routine 3 doses given at 0, 1, 6 months *or* Super-accelerated with 4 doses given at 0, 7, 21 days and final dose at 12 months

The amount of hepatitis A antigen contained in the combination vaccine is half that contained in the single dose vaccine. The two cannot therefore be substituted for each other within a course.

Hepatitis B

What is hepatitis B?

The term hepatitis B may be used to describe either the virus itself or the disease caused by the infection. Hep B or HBV are sometimes used as abbreviations.

HBV infection can cause acute and chronic illness. The majority of adults will not experience early symptoms and so infection can go unnoticed for a long period.

In adults infected with HBV, 90–95% will clear their bodies of the virus naturally. The remaining 5–10% will continue to be infected and be potentially infectious to others for the rest of their lives unless successfully treated to eradicate the virus.

How is it spread?

Hepatitis B is the most infectious of all the viruses discussed in this chapter. The virus is present in body fluids such as blood, saliva, semen and vaginal fluid.

In the UK, hepatitis B is mainly passed on from person to person by having unprotected sex or sharing injecting paraphernalia. In the rest of the world, the most common infection route is from infected mother to child, or from child to child.

Blood

- Contact with even a tiny amount of infected blood through an open wound or cut or scratch may cause infection.

- The virus can be transmitted through sharing injecting equipment for drug use. It is especially important to highlight that any paraphernalia may carry infection, i.e. water, filters, work surfaces.

- The virus can be transmitted through use of infected equipment in dental, medical, tattooing or acupuncture procedures.

- Receiving a blood transfusion in countries where blood is not screened for infection may cause infection.

Sex

- Sexual intercourse is one of the most common routes of transmission in the UK.

- People with multiple sexual partners have an increased risk of exposure to the virus.

- Any sexual activity that presents a risk of blood to blood contact will carry a greater risk of transmission, e.g. sex during menstruation, anal sex, or in the presence of another sexually transmitted disease.

- The virus can be transmitted through oral sex.

Mother to baby

- Without treatment, 90% of babies born to infected mothers will develop chronic infection.

- With treatment for the baby, i.e. giving immunoglobulin and commencing vaccination within 12 hours of birth, the risk of transmission becomes less than 5%.

- Breastfeeding carries a risk of transmission if the baby is untreated but is safe once vaccination has been commenced.

NB Since April 2000, all pregnant women in the UK are offered routine screening for hepatitis B.

What happens when a person is infected?

Incubation period

After infection with the virus it can take one to six months for symptoms to appear. The majority of those infected will not suffer acute symptoms and will therefore remain unaware of their infection.

Diagnosis

A blood test for hepatitis B surface antigen (**HBsAg** – a protein from the virus) will confirm the diagnosis. A number of other antigen and antibody tests can be carried out to confirm how long the infection has been present and how the body is responding to the infection.

Antibodies

A blood test for hepatitis B surface antigen antibodies (**anti-HBs**) indicates immunity either because of resolved past infection or due to previous vaccination. In both cases these antibodies protect against re-infection.

Acute hepatitis B

All or none of the symptoms of acute hepatitis may be present.

This is the type of viral hepatitis most likely to lead to severe acute illness requiring hospital admission and in rare cases an urgent liver transplant.

Most commonly, however, any acute symptoms will clear within weeks or at most a few months. There is no specific treatment for acute hepatitis B. Sufferers need rest, fluids and a healthy diet. It is best to avoid alcohol and certain prescribed drugs.

If the infection is diagnosed in the acute stages, the Public Health Department will be notified and will advise on testing and vaccination of sexual and household contacts.

Chronic hepatitis B

Hepatitis B is called chronic when the infection lasts longer than six months. A blood test for HBsAg confirms the virus is present. While this antigen remains in the body the person has the potential to infect others and is sometimes referred to as a 'carrier'. Most carriers remain infectious, but a small number get rid of the virus after several years.

Chronic hepatitis B can run two courses, which are:

- chronic persistent hepatitis, where the virus persists but causes minimal liver damage

- chronic active hepatitis, where there is aggressive destruction of liver tissue and rapid progression to liver disease. Some individuals will develop primary liver cancer because of their infection.

Treatment

People with chronic hepatitis B should be referred to a specialist liver disease unit or infectious disease unit where the degree of liver damage can be assessed. Not everyone will be suitable for treatment but monitoring every 6–12 months for disease progression is advisable.

If treatment is needed, combinations of drugs can be used, including interferon and lamivudine. These treatments do not work for everybody and side effects can make it difficult to tolerate them. Clinical trials are available at many specialist centres looking at different combinations of drugs to improve outcomes.

Key prevention issues

Infected individuals should be made aware that there is a risk to those who live with them. Household contacts should be vaccinated, and if the infection is acute, offered immunoglobulin and vaccination, as the immunoglobulin offers earlier protection. There is no risk of infection from normal social contact such as touching or using a toilet seat. Therefore, occasional visitors and friends do not need vaccination.

To reduce the risk of infecting others, infected individuals should:

- carefully clean and cover cuts, scratches and open wounds with waterproof plasters
- clean up blood from floors and work surfaces with undiluted household bleach
- never share personal items such as toothbrushes, razors, scissors
- use condoms when having sex to protect their partner
- never share injecting equipment when taking drugs and make sure surfaces for preparing drugs are cleaned with bleach.

Vaccination

Hepatitis B disease can be prevented by vaccination.

Low prevalence of hepatitis B in the general population in the UK (around 0.2%) has made the government reluctant to introduce a vaccination programme across the whole population. In 1988, the government instead recommended a policy that targeted high-risk groups for vaccination.

The implementation of this policy for injecting drug users – recognised to be one of the groups at high risk – has been poor and regional implementation plans still vary enormously. A number of initiatives, including the additional funding from the Department of Health in England and Wales to improve rates of vaccination for injecting drug users and the National Enhanced Service for patients with drug misuse problems (new GP contract), may see the situation improve.

Because of these regional variations, local arrangements should be checked before advising clients. Some areas may only be offering vaccination to injecting drug users, whilst others vaccinate all drug users. Local Public Health Consultants will be able to tell drug workers the arrangements that have been made for their area.

The venues likely to offer vaccination to drug users are GP surgeries, specialist drug services, harm reduction/needle exchange schemes or genito-urinary medicine clinics.

Vaccine schedules

Testing blood for HBV is not essential before commencing vaccination, as no harm will result from vaccinating someone who has already been exposed to the virus. The ideal situation would be to take a blood test and administer the first dose of vaccine at the same appointment. This would have three possible advantages:

- the opportunity to commence vaccination will not have been missed.

- if the person is HBsAg positive, indicating they are currently infected, they can be directed to treatment and no further vaccination doses are required.

- if the person is positive for antibodies to hepatitis B (anti-HBs), indicating pre-existing immunity, no further vaccination doses are required.

Three possible vaccination schedules for hepatitis B are licensed in the UK. The schedule which best fits with routine contact arrangements for seeing the drug user is most likely to succeed in delivering a full course. Even incomplete courses will offer some protection against disease.

Hepatitis B vaccination schedules

Routine	Injections given at 0, 1 and 6 months
Accelerated	Injections given at 0, 1, 2 and 12 months
Super-accelerated	Injections given at 0, 7, 21 days and 12 months

Post-vaccination antibody testing

A blood test may be carried out two to four months after the last injection of the vaccination course to ensure adequate immunity has been achieved. This blood test will measure the amount of hepatitis B antibody present.

In healthy adults, 5–10% will not mount an effective antibody response after vaccination and people with a damaged immune system (e.g. due to HIV infection) may be at higher risk of not responding. It is, nonetheless, likely that even these apparent non-responders will gain some benefit from vaccination by developing less extreme forms of the illness if they become exposed to the virus at a later date.

Booster doses may be offered to people who respond poorly to the initial vaccine course.

2

Hepatitis C

What is hepatitis C?

The term hepatitis C may be used to describe either the virus itself or the disease caused by the infection. Hep C or HCV are sometimes used as abbreviations.

Hepatitis C can cause either an acute or chronic illness. The acute illness may produce flu-like symptoms, occasionally with nausea, vomiting and jaundice, but this is unusual and HCV is rarely diagnosed at the acute stage of infection.

Following acute infection, 20–50% of people will clear the virus and make a natural recovery. It is not known why some people are successful at fighting off the infection.

The remaining 50–80% will have chronic hepatitis C infection and, if untreated, have an increased risk of liver disease and primary liver cancer.

How is it spread?

In the UK, of the 60,000 reported cases known to be HCV antibody positive at the end of 2003, over 90% were associated with injecting drug use as the risk factor for transmission. More than two in five in injecting drug users (IDUs) have been infected with HCV.

Although uptake of testing for HCV among IDUs has increased in recent years, it is estimated that around half of IDUs with HCV remain unaware of their infection.

Blood

- Contact with even a tiny amount of infected blood through an open wound, cut or scratch may cause infection.

- The virus can be transmitted through sharing injecting equipment and paraphernalia for drug use. It is especially important to highlight that any paraphernalia may carry infection, i.e. water, filters, work surfaces.

- In the UK, all blood donations have been screened for hepatitis C since 1991, but people who received blood or blood products before then may have been infected. Some countries still do not screen blood and blood products for this virus and treatment within their boundaries may still carry a risk of infection.

- The virus can be transmitted through use of infected equipment in dental, medical, tattooing or acupuncture procedures.

Sex

- Heterosexual transmission of hepatitis C is possible. However, transmission has been found to be rare in monogamous heterosexual couples and it may be reasonable for them to choose not to change their sexual practices.

- Any sexual activity which risks blood-to-blood contact, e.g. sex during menstruation, anal sex, or the presence of another sexually transmitted disease will carry greater risk.

- A number of outbreaks of acute hepatitis C in men who have sex with men have been reported. Factors increasing the likelihood of transmission in these cases were:

  - pre-existing HIV disease

  - passive anal receptive sex

  - the presence of another sexually transmitted disease.

Mother to baby

- There are no current treatments proven to reduce the transmission rate between an infected woman and her baby.

- Of babies born to HCV infected women, 6% will become infected. It is not known whether infection occurs in the womb, during delivery or immediately after the birth.

- There is no evidence of transmission by breastfeeding, which is considered to be safe.

NB Women are not routinely screened for HCV during pregnancy, as there are no available treatments to affect outcomes. Ribavirin, a mainstay of treatment for HCV, is teratogenic (risks damaging the unborn child) and so cannot be taken during pregnancy. Women who have a history of injecting drug use should be counselled regarding the possibility of being tested at this time, as there may be advantages in knowing about infection to ensure follow-up care for the mother and child.

What happens when a person is infected?

Incubation period

There is no clear incubation period as HCV has so far rarely been studied in the acute phase.

Diagnosis

A blood test for antibodies to HCV (**anti-HCV**) may be taken either because previous risk is identified or, less commonly, because symptoms of the disease are present. The period between possible risk of infection and antibodies appearing can be between two to six months. This is sometimes referred to as the 'window' period and blood tests taken within this time may give a false negative result and should be repeated.

A positive antibody test indicates you have been exposed to the virus. A further PCR (polymerase chain reaction) test is required to test for the presence of the virus itself. This test is usually automatically carried out on the same blood sample by the laboratory.

A positive PCR test indicates active infection. This group of people should be referred to a specialist for advice and possible treatment.

People testing positive for antibodies but negative for PCR have cleared the virus and will not require treatment.

Antibodies

Because HCV mutates at a rapid rate, these antibodies do not protect against the possibility of future infection with another strain of HCV.

Acute hepatitis C

All or none of the symptoms of acute hepatitis may be present, but most commonly there are no significant early symptoms. Outbreaks of acute hepatitis C infection have been reported from some HIV treatment centres in the UK since the introduction of routine screening for HCV in this patient population. In these cases, up to 50% of people have been able to clear the virus naturally. The course of this disease in its early stages is still poorly understood.

Chronic hepatitis C

Hepatitis C is described as chronic when the infection lasts longer than six months. A PCR test will confirm if the virus is present. Further blood tests can be carried out at specialist treatment centres, which will identify the strain of HCV causing the infection. This is called the genotype. HCV has six main genotypes, numbered 1 to 6. Genotypes 1, 2 and 3 are the most common types found in the UK. The genotype does not seem to influence the course of the disease but is important in predicting the likely response to treatment. Genotype 1 requires a longer course of treatment (12 months) and can be less likely to achieve a successful treatment outcome.

Presence of the virus indicates the person has the potential to infect others.

Many people who are chronically infected can expect to live out their normal lifespan. However, 5–20% may over the course of 10 to 30 years develop symptoms of serious liver disease. A small proportion of these will develop primary liver cancer. Factors such as being male, aged over 40 years at time of infection, having a high alcohol intake and co-infection with hepatitis B or HIV have all been associated with more rapid progress of the disease. Doctors are unable to predict who will or will not go on to develop serious liver disease as a consequence of HCV infection.

Symptoms of chronic disease can include:

- mild to severe fatigue

- anxiety

- weight loss

- loss of appetite

- alcohol intolerance

- pain in the area of the liver

- concentration problems

- feeling sick

- flu-like symptoms such as fevers, chills, night sweats and headaches

- jaundice.

These symptoms may come and go over time and are unrelated to the level of liver disease present. It is not unusual for people to be misdiagnosed with chronic fatigue syndrome or ME if their medical practitioner is not alert to the risk of hepatitis C.

Treatment

People with chronic hepatitis C should be referred to a specialist liver disease unit or infectious disease unit for assessment and treatment.

In most centres, liver biopsy is no longer required as part of the routine assessment. This very uncomfortable procedure was credited with putting off many patients coming in for assessment. Liver biopsy may still be helpful in allowing the specialist to assess the level of liver damage. This may then allow the infected individual to make an informed choice about the urgency for treatment.

2

Treatment is with a combination of pegylated interferon alpha (by weekly injection) and ribavirin (twice-daily tablets). These drugs are given together for six or 12 months depending on the genotype and other prognostic factors.

The main aim of treatment is to achieve a sustained viral response (SVR). This means that blood tests carried out six months after finishing the course of treatment show no detectable virus; 20–80% of people completing treatment will achieve an SVR. The poorer response to treatment is influenced by:

- having genotype 1 infection
- being over 40 years of age
- being male
- having higher levels of virus present pre-treatment.

Because experience of this treatment is relatively new most individuals will be followed for a longer period than six months post-treatment, but it is expected that having achieved an SVR they will require no further treatment and have been effectively cured. A very small number of cases may relapse at a later time and knowledge of the long-term treatment experience over 10 to 30 years is still in its infancy.

Key prevention issues

- HCV prevalence has been estimated to be as high as 80% in some drug using communities. This means the likelihood of infection for a person who is sharing their injecting equipment can be very high.

- HCV is more robust than HIV and the risks of transmission from sharing other injecting paraphernalia such as spoons, filters and water are significantly higher.

- Normal social contact does not carry any risk of infection, but the usual precautions should be taken to avoid sharing personal items such as razors, scissors and toothbrushes, which may carry the risk of blood-to-blood contact.

- Condom use will protect against sexual transmission.

Vaccination

There is no vaccination available for hepatitis C.

Human immunodeficiency virus (HIV)

What is HIV?

The term HIV describes the human immunodeficiency virus, which attacks the body's immune system, making it difficult to fight off infections. Once infected with the virus, an individual will remain infected for the rest of his/her life.

What is AIDS?

AIDS, or acquired immune deficiency syndrome, applies to the most advanced stages of HIV infection. The CDC (Center for Disease Control in Atlanta) originally developed the definition of AIDS and is responsible for tracking the spread of the disease in the USA. The CDC definition of AIDS includes:

- HIV-positive people who have a CD4 count of less than 200 (CD4 cells are one of the key mechanisms our immune systems use to fight infection, and healthy adults usually have CD4 counts in excess of 1,000), *or*

- HIV positive people who have suffered one of 26 clinical conditions known as AIDS-defining illnesses. These clinical conditions are usually opportunistic infections that generally do not cause disease in healthy people, or cancers such as Kaposi's sarcoma, cervical cancer or lymphomas.

The traditional CDC definition of AIDS attempted to classify stages of the disease depending on the types of infection or cancers that were occurring, in order to give a general idea of how sick a person had become. With improved treatment of HIV disease, these classifications are becoming obsolete as they no longer reflect the progression of the disease.

How is it spread?

In the UK the most commonly reported route of transmission is through sexual contact. In the early 1990s large numbers of IDUs were infected, but the introduction of harm reduction policies such as needle exchange schemes and methadone maintenance programmes have been credited with the drastic reduction of new cases reporting this as their route of transmission. The behaviour, however, of sharing injecting equipment has not shown a steady decline and the potential for transmission remains.

Blood

- The virus can be transmitted through sharing injecting equipment for drug use.

2

- Since 1985, in the UK, all blood and tissue donations have been screened and heat-treated to eliminate HIV. People who received blood or blood products before this time in the UK may have been infected.

- Receiving treatment involving blood or blood products in countries where blood is not screened for this virus continues to carry a risk.

Sex

- Heterosexual transmission is now the leading route of transmission reported in the UK. A considerable number of these cases will have contracted the virus abroad.

- Homosexual transmission continues to be a major route of infection.

- Oral sex can transmit the virus.

Mother to baby

- Without treatment, 15–20% of babies born to infected women will develop the infection.

- With treatment, the risk can be reduced to less than 1%. Treatment may involve:

  - antiretroviral treatment for the woman in pregnancy

  - antiretroviral treatment for the woman during delivery and a short course of treatment for the baby at birth

  - Caesarean section delivery.

- Breastfeeding is known to carry the risk of transmission and should be avoided.

NB Since April 2000, all pregnant women in the UK are offered screening for HIV.

What happens when a person is infected?

Incubation period

A small number of people experience a flu-like illness one to two months after being infected. The majority of people suffer no early symptoms.

Diagnosis

A blood test for HIV antibodies will confirm the diagnosis. It can take up to three months after infection for antibodies to appear. This is sometimes referred to as the 'window' period and blood tests taken within this time may give a false negative result and should be repeated.

Antibodies

There are many different strains of HIV. Antibodies produced in reaction to one strain will not be protective against re-infection by a different strain.

Acute HIV infection

This illness may include:

- fever

- sore throat

- headaches

- tiredness

- enlarged lymph nodes (glands of the immune system easily felt in the neck and groin).

These symptoms usually disappear within one to four weeks of onset and are often mistaken for those of a non-specific viral illness with flu-like symptoms. This is commonly referred to as a sero-conversion illness. HIV is present in large quantities in blood and genital fluids at this stage making people highly infectious.

Chronic HIV disease

More persistent or severe symptoms may not appear for five to ten years after the initial infection. This period of asymptomatic infection varies greatly in each individual. Even during this asymptomatic period the virus will continue to damage the immune system. HIV infection is always for life.

It is this damage to the immune system that can in itself cause moderate symptoms, but more importantly makes the individual vulnerable to opportunistic infections which can be life threatening.

The early symptoms related to immune damage include:

- lack of energy
- weight loss
- frequent fevers and sweats
- persistent or frequent yeast infections (oral or vaginal)
- persistent skin rashes or flaky skin
- pelvic inflammatory disease in women that does not respond to treatment
- short-term memory loss
- severe herpes infections that cause mouth, genital or anal sores
- shingles.

People with AIDS may suffer a range of symptoms, depending on the opportunistic infection they are affected by. Drug users, especially if they are known to be HIV positive, should be encouraged to seek medical help if any of the following symptoms appear:

- persistent cough over several weeks
- fever
- sweats
- extreme shortness of breath which is getting worse
- severe and sudden weight loss
- vision loss.

Treatment

Without treatment, people with HIV infection will experience a progressive decline in their health. This progression can be insidious at first, with periods of feeling well between health problems that may not initially be associated with HIV infection. The speed of this decline is highly variable and is fatal if untreated.

This course of the disease should rarely be experienced in the UK today, as effective treatment is available. Treatment of HIV disease is highly specialised and needs to be directly provided or supervised by a specialist. Specialists usually work in infectious disease units or genito-urinary medicine departments.

The introduction in 1996 of Highly Active Anti-Retroviral Treatment (HAART), or combination therapy, has dramatically changed the expected outcome for someone infected with HIV. HAART is a combination of three to four drugs that treat the HIV infection and stop the virus from replicating. It can be a complicated treatment to adhere to and at the moment it is expected that an individual would need to remain in treatment for the rest of his/her life. However, this form of treatment introduced for the first time the possibility that people with HIV infection could hope to live out their normal lifespan.

NB Some of the drugs used in the treatment of HIV disease are known to interact with and inhibit the effect of methadone and some forms of oral contraception.

Key prevention issues

- HIV prevalence in drug using communities is now low; it is estimated at 3.6% in London and 0.2% for the rest of England and Wales. Around 100 new cases are identified each year, however, and new transmissions are still occurring.

- Clients who inject drugs abroad should be reminded that many European countries have higher prevalence rates than the UK in their drug using communities. Two-thirds of IDUs diagnosed in 2002 in England and Wales had acquired their infections abroad, mostly in southern Europe.

Vaccination

There is no vaccination currently available.

Co-infection

Co-infection with any combination of the hepatitis and HIV viruses is possible and is likely to worsen the prognosis for the individual. Specific studies into exactly how co-infection will influence the course of each infection are few and sometimes contradictory in their results. A brief summary of current knowledge is given below.

Hepatitis C and HIV

- Hepatitis C does not seem to cause a more aggressive course of HIV-related disease.

- Advanced HIV disease makes it more likely that HCV-related liver cirrhosis will occur and progress more quickly to End Stage Liver Disease (ESLD) than in those infected with hepatitis C alone. ESLD is now a major cause of death in people with HIV.

- Co-infected people have comparably higher rates of HCV viraemia (high levels of virus in the blood), which is likely to have a negative impact on health outcomes.

- Co-infected people appear to be more infectious to others, although the exact reason for this is unknown. Co-infected mothers are more likely to pass HCV on to their children at birth, and sexual transmission risk for HCV may be increased with co-infected men showing higher levels of HCV in semen.

- The presence of both infections can make treatment more difficult. Many HIV drug treatments carry a risk of liver inflammation, and blood monitoring is extremely important. Treatment is best carried out in a centre with experience of treating both infections and priority will usually be given to treating the most advanced disease first. Co-infection should not be a barrier to entering treatment for either disease.

Hepatitis C and hepatitis B

In theory the presence of these two viruses should cause more damage at a faster rate, but the evidence from research is still lacking. It is recommended that hepatitis C positive people should be vaccinated against hepatitis B to prevent the risk of this co-infection.

Hepatitis C and hepatitis A

People with chronic hepatitis C are at particular risk of life-threatening episodes of fulminant hepatitis if they are exposed to hepatitis A. Hepatitis A vaccination is recommended for HCV-positive individuals for this reason.

General prevention messages

A harm reduction approach to people who take illicit drugs has been adopted in the UK since the Advisory Council on the Misuse of Drugs (1988) advised the government that, 'The threat to individual and public health posed by HIV and AIDS was much greater than the threat posed by drug misuse.'

The harm reduction message generated to avoid the spreading of HIV in drug users needs to be adapted and re-invigorated to tackle the much more prevalent HCV epidemic. The essential message remains the same.

- Avoid injecting drugs if possible.

- If you are going to inject drugs, do so as safely as possible.

- Do not share any injecting equipment, including needles, syringes, water, filters and swabs.

- The more times a person is exposed to these viruses the greater the risk that they will become infected. Therefore, cutting down the frequency of sharing is helpful – but just once might be enough to become infected.

- Cleaning the needle and syringe with diluted bleach is not guaranteed to get rid of HBV or HCV, but it is still worthwhile if there is no alternative to sharing.

- Try to find a clean surface to prepare the hit.

- Avoid touching anything that may be contaminated with someone else's blood.

- Try to wash your hands before preparing a hit.

Using a condom is an extremely effective way to avoid infection with all of these viruses as well as many other sexually transmitted diseases.

Useful websites

England and Wales Health Protection Agency www.hpa.org.uk

Health Protection Scotland www.hps.scot.nhs.uk

British Liver Trust www.britishlivertrust.org.uk

National Institute for Clinical Excellence (NICE) www.nice.org.uk

NAM Aidsmap www.aidsmap.com

British HIV Association (BHIVA) www.bhiva.org

3 | Working with service users under the age of 18

This chapter provides basic guidance and information on the responsibilities of drug and alcohol workers in relation to service users who are under the age of 18. It may be of particular relevance for workers in services for adults who from time to time come into contact with under-18s.

Principles for working with young people under 18

Teenagers can seem very mature but do not be tempted to treat them as adults. The needs of young people who misuse drugs and alcohol are different from those of adults and, ideally, services for them should be provided separately from those for adults. Staff working with young people should be trained to understand their developmental and emotional needs as well as the range of legal and ethical issues which do not apply when working with adults.

The Children Act 1989, the Children Act 2004 and the Children (Scotland) Act 1995 set out the legal framework within which substance misuse workers and other professionals working with young people operate. The basic principles are the same and are drawn from the 1989 United Nations Convention on the Rights of the Child, ratified by the UK in 1991.

Good practice principles

The following principles for working with service users under the age of 18 are taken from those drawn up by the Children's Legal Centre and the Standing Conference on the Abuse of Drugs (1999).

- **A child (or young person under the age of 18) is not an adult.**

- **The best interests of the child should be the paramount concern of professionals working with them.**

- **The wishes and feelings of the child should always be taken into account.** Workers should always seek and listen to a child's views and opinions, and give them weight according to their age and maturity. If a decision is taken which goes against the child's expressed wishes, this should be discussed with them.

- **Services need to respect parental responsibility.** The involvement, support and education of parents and legal guardians are likely to promote successful working with young people, and a parent's permission may be necessary before providing a service to a young person.

- **Services should recognise the role of, and co-operate with the local authority** in carrying out its responsibilities towards children and young people who are 'in need' or who may be 'suffering, or at risk of suffering, significant harm'.

- **Services should be child-centred, take a holistic approach and respond to the individual needs of the young person.** Staff working in young people's drug and alcohol services should be competent to work with children, adolescents and families from different ethnic minorities and with substance misuse. They should be able to respond to complex individual, family and cultural needs and to take a multi-disciplinary and cross-agency approach when needed. Services for young people should be provided separately from those for adults.

Assessment

Government guidance emphasises the importance of early assessments of vulnerable children and young people in order to make an effective intervention. Whenever a young person under 18 attends a substance misuse service, a member of staff needs to assess whether the young person is experiencing, or at risk of, 'significant harm'. This should form part of the initial assessment of a young person's needs, which must be carried out before it is decided whether to recommend treatment or other intervention.

Consent to treatment

Different treatment options should be explained to the young person and where possible to their parents. Young people aged 16 to 18 are able to consent to their own treatment, except for extreme circumstances such as a severe learning disability. Normally, for young people under 16, a parent or legal guardian needs to consent to their treatment. However, where a parent is not available and the young person will not agree to their being contacted, under 16s may be competent to consent to their own treatment.

Parent's or parental responsibility holder's[1] consent

- It is good practice to consult and keep both parents informed (if they are involved with the child) unless there are valid reasons for not doing so.

- It is only necessary to obtain the permission of one parent or other parental responsibility holder.

- One person with parental responsibility cannot veto the consent of the other parent. However, the objecting parent could seek a court order to prevent treatment. The situation may be complex where parental responsibility is shared between a local authority and a parent.

- A parent who consents to treatment – e.g. counselling – does not need to be informed of what the child said in the counselling session unless the child explicitly consents.

- A parent can withdraw consent to treatment at any time, and the treatment must stop unless the child consents to it continuing and is competent to do so.

Assessing a young person's competence to consent to treatment

There are no hard and fast rules for deciding whether a young person under 16 can consent to their own treatment, but the following factors should be considered:

- the age and maturity of the child, which must be assessed individually

- the child's understanding of their actions

- the child's understanding of the consequences of treatment

- the extent to which their understanding may be affected by factors such as intoxication by drugs or alcohol, or learning difficulties

- the nature and level of treatment – the level of competence needed to consent to counselling, for example, is likely to be lower than that to consent to needle exchange.

---

1 An unmarried father does not automatically have parental responsibility for his child in the eyes of the law. However any person who has care of a child (for example a relative) may do "what is reasonable in all the circumstances of the case for the purpose of safeguarding or promoting the child's welfare", including consent to treatment on their behalf. It is unlikely that a court would agree that it would be reasonable for someone without parental responsibility to take a decision to which the parental responsibility holder would object.

3

Sixteen- and 17-year-olds are usually considered able to consent to treatment, but even for this age group their competence should be fully assessed, and it is good practice to involve parents wherever possible.

Every agency working with under-18s should have guidelines on consent to treatment and staff should receive specialist training on assessing young people's competence to give consent.

In practice, for the treatment to be effective, it may be vital for a young person to consent to treatment irrespective of their age.

> 'If we felt a young person wasn't competent to consent to their own treatment, we wouldn't work with them. Generally though, the fact that they have come to the service is an indication of their level of maturity. Often young people are sent to us by their parents. It's difficult for us to work with chaotic users who aren't motivated to change. To be able to benefit from treatment young people need a capacity to reflect.' Counsellor working in young people's drug and alcohol service

Fraser Guidelines

When agencies talk about the assessment they make as to whether a young person can be provided with confidential health services without parental consent, they often refer to the *Fraser Guidelines*. These guidelines arise from the case in the early 1980s when Victoria Gillick attempted to set a legal precedent in England and Wales which would have prevented medical practitioners from giving young people under the age of 16 contraceptive advice or treatment without parental permission.

The House of Lords ruled that **people under 16 who are fully able to understand what is proposed and its implications, are competent to consent to medical treatment regardless of age.** This is now the legal position in England and Wales. In Scotland, the ruling has also been interpreted as meaning that medical practitioners can give advice or treatment to young people under 16 without parental knowledge.

The Fraser guidelines suggest that before providing a service to under-16s to which parents have not given consent the staff member should ensure that the following criteria are met:

- The young person understands the advice being given.

- The young person cannot be convinced to involve parents/carers or allow the medical practitioner to do so on his/her behalf.

- It is likely that the young person will begin or continue having intercourse with or without treatment/contraception.

- Unless the young person receives treatment/contraception, his/her physical or mental health (or both) is likely to suffer.

- The young person's best interests require contraceptive advice to be given without parental consent.

In making his judgement, Lord Fraser, provided a set of criteria which must apply when medical practitioners are offering contraceptive services to under 16s without parental knowledge or permission. The so-called Fraser Guidelines (some people refer to assessing whether the young person is Gillick competent) state that all the following requirements should be fulfilled. Most agencies offering information, advice or services to young people about their health have adopted the Fraser Guidelines as the basis for best practice.

Young people with a physical or learning disability have the same right to appropriate confidential advice and treatment as any other young person. They may have particular individual needs which will have to be considered, but their rights to services remain the same.

Where an agency cannot provide the service needed by the young person, it is within the law for the agency to provide information and/or to make an appointment or accompany the young person to another agency which can meet his/her requirements, and to do this without parental knowledge.

Scottish law on consent

The Age of Legal Capacity (Scotland) Act 1991 assigns various legal rights to people over the age of 12 but, as in England and Wales, there is no minimum age for legal capacity to consent to medical treatment. People under 16 are legally able to consent on their own behalf to any surgical, medical or dental procedure or treatment if, in the doctor's opinion, they are capable of understanding the nature and possible consequences of the procedure. Clearly, the more serious the medical procedure proposed, a correspondingly better grasp of the implications is required.

Confidentiality

Like any other service user, a person under the age of 18 attending drug and alcohol treatment services has a right to expect confidentiality. However, no agency can guarantee absolute confidentiality. Where you have concerns that a young person is suffering from, or is at risk of, significant harm you have a duty to contact child protection services.

Different agencies operate with different levels of confidentiality. Some services wish to guarantee complete confidentiality except where there are concerns about significant harm. Your agency's confidentiality policy should be explained to a young person before they are assessed and, if appropriate, reiterated.

If you decide it is within a client's best interests to share information with a parent or another agency and this is within your agency's policy on confidentiality, wherever possible you should get the young person's agreement first. Passing on information gained in confidence without a young person's agreement is a breach of trust and is likely to result in them disengaging from the service.

Key points

The following points should be considered when deciding whether to disclose confidential information without a young person's consent.

- **The age and maturity of the child** Legally, there is no minimum age to the right to confidentiality. However, with younger children there is a risk that failure to inform parents could lead to them successfully suing an agency for not doing enough to protect a child from harm as a result of substance misuse. It is unlikely, for example, that a service could provide treatment for a child under 13 without parental agreement.

- **The seriousness of the substance misuse** In deciding whether to pass on information, you need to consider the seriousness of the substance misuse and the risks of significant physical and mental harm, and the likelihood of substance misuse continuing or escalating. You also need to consider risks of involvement in crime and whether the young person is being exploited or abused by the supplier.

- **Context of the substance misuse** Young people who come to a drug or alcohol treatment service may have other problems in their lives and may benefit from support from other services to reduce their vulnerability. They may be experiencing abuse, estranged from their parents or homeless, or they may have run away from care. Workers should encourage young people in such circumstances to get involved with other relevant support services.

Where the young person disagrees with information being passed on, you should assess the young person's circumstances before deciding whether to contact their parents, child protection or other services against their wishes.

'If you disclose against a young person's wishes, you break their trust. People won't come to us [for counselling] if they feel that they can't control things. We only ever break confidentiality for child protection or risk to others. Ninety-nine times out of a hundred you can work with a client and get their agreement to passing on information.' Manager in young people's counselling service.

Information sharing

There are many instances when it is in a young person's best interests to contact other agencies involved with them – for example, to agree their care plan with a GP or mental health professional. Government guidance emphasises the importance of multi-agency working and good information sharing between agencies, including health, housing, education and social services to ensure that a young person has all their needs considered.

Children and young people who misuse substances often have complex problems and may benefit from support from their parents or from referral to other services. All agencies working with young people should have protocols for liaising with parents, child protection, health and education, youth offending teams and other relevant services.

All conversations with a young client about information sharing should be recorded. The record should include not only *whom* the information will be shared with, but *what* information and *why*. Some agencies have a policy of obtaining the young person's written consent before information is passed on.

There is no need to inform parents or social services if a young person approaches a service for information, basic advice or onward referral, as children are entitled to seek such information without the consent of a parent.

3

'We work closely with GPs [and other professionals]. I make clear to clients right at the beginning that this is how we work, but I also tell them if I'm intending to get in touch with their GP and get their consent.' Psychiatric nurse working in drug service

Child protection

Substance misuse by young people under the age of 18 may give rise to concerns that they are suffering significant harm. Child protection concerns affecting young drug users range from harm through overdose, injecting, blood-borne viruses, etc. to exposure to emotional and/or sexual abuse or exploitation.

Drug and alcohol services have a duty[2] to communicate concerns that a child may be 'suffering, or at risk of suffering, significant harm' to local child protection services. All agencies should have a written child protection policy setting out procedures to be followed if child protection concerns arise. This should be consistent with local area child protection guidelines and be drawn up in consultation with local child protection services. All members of staff need to be fully trained on the implications for their work.

Young drug users are often extremely vulnerable and reluctant to trust adults or engage with services, and you may be concerned that if you disclose information to other agencies they will withdraw from the service. These legitimate concerns do not mean that drugs and alcohol workers can sidestep legal requirements.

If a young person is referred by another agency or professional, you should not assume that child protection is already being taken care of. Child protection must be an ongoing priority for everyone working with under 18s who are misusing substances. A young person's situation may be volatile and change quickly, or the young person may disclose new information.

In deciding whether to contact child protection services, you need to consider the degree of risk to the young person and take account of their age and maturity. Child protection issues are often very complex and it is ultimately for local child protection services to decide whether a child is at risk and what action should be taken. If you have concerns about any child or young person, the first step should be to discuss the case with a nominated child protection officer, or, if your agency does not have one with a child protection adviser in the local authority. Unless it would put the child at further risk, you should inform the service user that you intend to do so.

2 Child protection legislation varies between England, Scotland, Wales and Northern Ireland and a drug worker's precise legal responsibility may depend on whom they are employed by and the contractual relationship between their employer and the statutory services.

For further discussion of child protection issues, refer to the chapter on children of substance misusing parents.

Children and young people's databases (identification, retrieval and tracking)

In England and Wales new legal provisions are being introduced under the Children Act 2004 to establish local information systems for sharing information about children with the aim of promoting their welfare. The provisions originate from the government Green Paper *Every Child Matters* and from concerns highlighted by Lord Laming's inquiry into the death of Victoria Climbié that there was a failure to share concerns about her welfare between different agencies.

Government guidance highlights the role of integrated information systems to help agencies work together to track interventions with individual children and young people.

At the time of going to press, the details of the new information systems had not yet been agreed. Different approaches may be adopted in different local areas. It is not clear how the new information-sharing provisions will affect agencies working with young people who misuse substances, but they are likely to have implications for confidentiality and information-sharing policies.

Young people 'looked after' by the local authority

Young people who are looked after by the local authority (ie, young people in care) may be at greater risk of misusing substances and less likely to have the benefit of protective personal and social factors, such as a close relationship with a parent or other responsible adult. The same issues of confidentiality, consent and information sharing arise for looked after young people as with other young people, except that the question arises as to who may consent to drug treatment.

Who may give consent to treatment for a looked after young person?

A young person aged over 16 is normally able to consent to their own treatment and this applies to young people who are looked after by a local authority. Where a young person is the subject of a care order, the local authority shares parental responsibility with the parents and may provide consent to drug or alcohol treatment. The local authority has the power to restrict a parent's exercise of parental responsibility where it is in a child's interests to do so, and can override a parent's refusal to give consent. In most cases, the care home or foster carer will be the primary legal guardian.

3

As a matter of good practice, the local authority should seek consent from the parents before treatment begins.

Harm reduction and needle exchanges

Providing needle exchange services for drug users under 18 is complex. Although the principle of reducing harm is still important, other considerations mean that services cannot be provided on an anonymous or minimal information basis as may be good practice in relation to adults. The following points need to be considered:

- Young people who inject drugs may be suffering, or at risk of suffering, significant harm, and child protection procedures should be followed.

- Every effort should be made to encourage young injectors to stop using drugs, stop injecting drugs or to enter drug treatment urgently.

- A risk assessment must be made before deciding whether to provide needle exchange in order to establish that *not* giving injecting equipment would pose a greater risk than that posed by continued, and possibly increased, injecting and recruiting others into injecting.

- An assessment of the young person's capacity to consent should be carried out and where possible parental consent obtained. If the young person is not assessed as being competent to consent and parents do not agree to treatment, the young person should not receive needle exchange.

- Ideally, a separate service should be provided for young people from that for older injectors. Minimal contact needle exchanges (e.g. pharmacy based) are not suitable and young people who approach such services should be referred to alternatives.

- In adult settings where no specific services for young people are available, protocols should be developed for harm reduction to young people.

Summary: Checklist of key procedures to be followed when working with clients under 18

- Young people attending any drug or alcohol service should be assessed immediately so that their needs can be identified fully and a care plan drawn up.

- A young person's capacity to consent to treatment should also be assessed.

- Treatment options should be explained to the client.

- The agency's confidentiality policy and criteria for breaching it should be explained.

- The client should be encouraged to agree to the involvement of parents or those with parental responsibility.

- Every agency should have a clear policy on the circumstances which would trigger the involvement of social services.

- The agency's policy on information-sharing with other agencies should be explained to the client, and their consent gained before information is shared.

References

British Medical Association, *Guidance from the ethics department: Parental responsibility*, September 2005 available online at www.bma.org.uk.

Children's Legal Centre and Standing Conference on Drug Abuse (1999) *Young People and Drugs: Policy guidance for drug interventions*

Department for Education and Skills (2005) *Every Child Matters: Change for children young people and drugs*

Department of Health and DrugScope (2002) *Taking Care with Drugs: Responding to substance misuse among looked after children*

4 Children of substance misusing parents

This chapter looks at the implications for children of parental drug and alcohol misuse and workers' responsibilities in relation to the children of clients. Traditionally, drug workers have not always regarded supporting clients in their parenting roles as part of their job. More recently, especially since the publication of *Hidden Harm* in 2003 (Advisory Council on the Misuse of Drugs), reducing harm to children is seen as a key task of professionals who work with people who misuse substances and drug agencies are taking on a greater role in promoting children's welfare.

Legislative context

The Children Act 1989, the Children Act 2004 and the Children (Scotland) Act 1995 set out the responsibilities of local authorities, health authorities and other agencies for promoting the welfare of children and protecting them from harm. The key principles underlying these Acts come from the 1989 United Nations Convention on the Rights of the Child. They include:

- all children have the right to be treated as individuals

- all children have the right to be protected from abuse, neglect and exploitation

- all children have the right to express their views on matters affecting them

- parents should normally be responsible for the upbringing of children and should share that responsibility

- public authorities and other agencies should promote the upbringing of children by their families so far as is consistent with safeguarding and promoting the child's well-being.

The Children Acts place local authorities under a duty to conduct an investigation if there are concerns that a child may be at risk of significant harm and to devise and implement a child protection plan. The Acts also require local authorities to provide services to support any child 'in need', defined as a child who is unlikely to achieve or maintain a reasonable standard of health and development, or whose health and development is likely to be impaired without the provision of services by a local authority. The Children Act 2004 imposes a new duty on authorities in England and Wales to co-operate with partner agencies to promote the well-being of children.

[handwritten margin note: Sig harm]

[handwritten note: promote partner working between agencies.]

4

Impact on children of parental substance misuse

Many parents with drug and alcohol problems do not neglect or abuse their children and manage to bring them up successfully. However, the more parents' lives focus on getting and using drugs, the more likely it is that children will be harmed. Because drug and alcohol use influences a person's state of mind and behaviour, the parent's attention to a child's basic needs and his/her perceptions, control of emotion, judgement and relationship to the child may all be affected.

Drug and alcohol workers need to be aware of the diversity of parenting roles, and the potential for children to be harmed through substance misuse by adults who are not their biological parents but nevertheless perform a parenting role. Substance misuse by a step-parent, grandparent, non-resident parent, older sibling or any adult with whom children have close contact can have a major impact on them.

Living with a parent or other adult whose drug use is chaotic and heavy (problem drug use) significantly increases a child's vulnerability to a wide range of adverse consequences. Their health, education, social relationships and emotional well-being may all be compromised. The effects are likely to be cumulative, with children at risk of developing social, emotional and psychological difficulties, underachieving in education and experiencing major difficulties and disadvantage in teenage and adult life, including becoming drug misusers themselves.

Dependent drug use by someone in a parenting role does not necessarily pose a threat to children, e.g. where a parent is stable on methadone. However, where the use is chaotic and illicit it is more likely that children will be harmed. Problem drug and alcohol use are frequently linked with other risk factors, including exposure to criminal behaviour, parental mental health problems, poverty, poor housing or homelessness, disrupted education, troubled family background and social isolation, all of which increase children's vulnerability.

A high proportion of the children of problem drug users do not live with one or both biological parents, or experience separation from them. Children may also experience the death of a parent through overdose, accident or suicide. Most children who do not live with either parent are looked after by relatives, but some are placed in care. If a child is living with relatives, they may still be exposed to risk of harm through contact with a substance misusing parent.

See Appendix 1 for further details of the potential impact on children's health and development of parental drug and alcohol misuse.

Effects of substance use on children

The ways in which parental substance use affects children depends on many factors, including whether:

- the substance use is stable or chaotic, which drug(s) a parent is using, how much and how often

- the parent is frequently intoxicated

- the drug use is illicit

- the substance use affects the quality of the parent's relationship with their child

- the child has close relationships with non-using relatives and other adults

- the parent only uses drugs when the child is not around and the child is safe when the parent is getting his/her drugs

- the child is exposed to adult criminal behaviour, violence or sexual activity

- parents play with their child, meet up with other (non-using) families and take them out

- the child's needs for regular meals, love and affection, clean clothes, toys and books, and school or preschool attendance are met

- the child is expected to take on too much responsibility for his/her age, e.g. looking after brothers and sisters or, in fact, the parents.

Protective factors which may mitigate harm

Although children may be harmed by their parents' substance misuse, some children do emerge relatively unscathed. Research shows that children and young people are more likely to be able to overcome adverse life events if they have:

- strong social support networks

- parents with a mutually supportive relationship and without high levels of conflict

- an unconditionally supportive relationship with at least one parent or parent substitute

- positive school experiences

4

- a committed mentor or other person outside the family

- involvement in the wider community.

Individual factors also make children either more resilient or more vulnerable. Characteristics which may *increase* a child's resilience include:

- sociability and an outgoing personality

- responsiveness to others

- a sense of humour

- the capacity to reflect on what has happened

- an easy temperament.

The harm to children and young people of parental substance misuse is likely to be reduced where:

- parents receive effective treatment

- one parent does not misuse substances

- other responsible adults are helpfully involved in the child's care

- family routines and activities are maintained

- the home is stable and safe with adequate financial resources.

However, all children of parents who misuse substances are potentially in need and possibly at risk, and none of these protective factors is a guarantee against harm.

Substance misuse during pregnancy

The harm to children of parental substance misuse may begin before birth, through the direct effect of the mother using drugs, alcohol and tobacco during pregnancy and the associated risk of poor diet and housing and inadequate antenatal care. Evidence of the direct effect of drugs on the unborn child is inconclusive, although a number of studies have shown increased risks of prematurity, SIDS (cot death) and low birthweight. Giving up drugs completely may not be a realistic option for a woman while she is pregnant. However, there are many steps a woman can take which will increase the chances of her having a normal pregnancy and a healthy baby. Drugs and alcohol workers can play an important role in supporting pregnant women by encouraging them to eat well, attend antenatal appointments and seek treatment for drug and alcohol problems.

Diet

Some of the documented harmful effects of maternal substance misuse during pregnancy may be due to poor maternal nutrition rather than the direct effects of drugs. Eating regular meals and a nutritionally balanced diet is essential for a healthy pregnancy.

Antenatal appointments

Pregnant women who misuse drugs or alcohol often fear they will be judged negatively by health professionals. They may also fear that child protection services will be informed automatically. However, good antenatal care makes a big difference to outcomes for pregnant women and their babies. Some areas provide specialist maternity services for women with drug and alcohol problems. Encouraging women to attend routine antenatal appointments is likely to be very beneficial and to increase the likelihood that potential problems are detected early on.

Tobacco

Many women who misuse drugs or alcohol also smoke heavily. Smoking during pregnancy reduces blood flow to the unborn child and increases the risk of miscarriage, SIDS (cot death), premature birth and low birthweight. Giving up smoking is one of the best things a pregnant woman can to do improve her baby's chances.

Alcohol

Heavy drinking and binge drinking are harmful during pregnancy. The Royal College of Gynaecologists and Obstetricians recommends that pregnant women should consume no more than one small drink a day. Frequent heavy drinking during pregnancy is linked to foetal alcohol syndrome, which may cause delayed neurological development, physical abnormalities, low IQ and problems with concentration and behaviour. Any woman who is unable to cut down her drinking or is dependent on alcohol should be referred to a specialist alcohol service.

Infant withdrawals

The babies of mothers who use opiates, benzodiazepines and alcohol when they are pregnant may suffer withdrawals at birth. However, babies can be treated successfully and the consensus amongst paediatricians and obstetricians is that it is safer for a woman to take a stable course of a prescribed opiate, such as methadone, than to use illicit opiates during pregnancy. Some GPs may try to get pregnant women to cut down on methadone, but this is generally poor advice as a woman may go into withdrawal.

4

Confidentiality, information sharing and child protection

Client confidentiality

Client confidentiality is a vital factor in enabling people to feel reassured about engaging with drug and alcohol services. People with drug and alcohol problems may fear that they will be stigmatised, blamed or refused help if other agencies are given information about them. They may also be worried about being investigated by the police about illegal drug use or that their children will be taken into care. Usually, drug workers can reassure clients that they can rely on agency staff to keep information confidential. However, child protection concerns are an important exception to this general rule.

The child's welfare is paramount. Where there are concerns that a child may be at risk of significant harm, this must always override requirements to keep information confidential.

Workers need to make it clear to clients that the welfare of children is the most important consideration in deciding whether to share information with others and that no agency can guarantee absolute confidentiality. Many agencies have a policy of confidentiality within the agency – i.e. where necessary discussing with colleagues issues which arise with individual clients. If this is your agency's policy you should explain to the client that it may sometimes be necessary to discuss issues to do with their case with a supervisor.

Where concerns about a child's safety or welfare require a worker to pass on confidential information, the client should be told that you intend to do so, unless you think this may put the child at greater risk of harm. You should also try to get the user to agree in advance to the sharing of necessary information.

> *'I worked with a woman who was very antagonistic and was threatening to run off with her child. I didn't tell her that I was going to inform child protection in case I might be placing the child at more risk.'* Community psychiatric nurse working in drug service

Assessment

> *'Because they are often the main agency in contact with problem drug using parents, all drug agencies should contribute to assessing and meeting the needs of their clients' children. This should be seen as an integral part of reducing drug-related harm … Gathering basic information about clients' children is an essential first step.'* Hidden Harm, ACMD 2003

Staff working in drug and alcohol services may be tempted to think that child protection is not their concern and that someone else will be looking out for the child. However, all agencies working with parents who misuse substances have a responsibility to gather information about children and to take action if they have concerns about their welfare. You should therefore ask about any children living with a client during their initial assessment.

Agencies vary in their ability to assess the needs of children and should agree with local child protection services how far they should probe in order to do this. If an initial assessment of a parent suggests that their substance misuse is likely to affect a child's health or development, or that the child is at risk of significant harm, you should follow your agency's child protection procedures.

You should also contact children and family social services or make a referral to appropriate local services if you believe a child of a client to be 'in need'. Local authorities also have a duty to provide services for children in their area who are in need, and most offer a range of services including advice, guidance and counselling, home helps and family centres. The support a local authority can give is dependent on their usually overstretched resources.

Information sharing

It is often necessary to share information with another agency such as health, housing or education services in order to best meet the client's and their children's needs. Liaising with the family health visitor is identified in *Hidden Harm* as a key task of drug agencies. For example, you may need to agree a client's care plan with their GP, health visitor, social worker or mental health worker and to keep everyone abreast of changes which arise in the client's or their children's circumstances. While it is good practice to share information on a 'need to know basis' with other professionals working with the family, this does not mean that personal details about the client need to be passed on.

When beginning work with a new client, a drug or alcohol worker should tell them as a matter of course about the agency's policy on information sharing and confidentiality, and explain the kinds of situations where it may be necessary to pass on information. Unless there are concerns about child protection or the safety of another person, the worker should *always* obtain the client's consent before passing on any information or making a referral. In order to engage with the service and trust staff, it is important that the client knows he/she has control over information sharing and can withdraw their consent at any time.

It is good practice to keep a record of the information to be shared, with whom and why, and to ask the client to sign it.

4

'A lot of the clients we see are also seeing psychiatrists or social workers. Sometimes it's in the client's interest for us to talk to another professional about something which comes up, but we would never do so without their consent unless it was child protection or someone was seriously threatening to stab their mother ... In 99 cases out of 100 you can work with a client and get their consent to share information outside the agency.' Counsellor in drug and alcohol service

'We work as part of a multidisciplinary team. I ask clients for the name of their health visitor, GP and social worker, or criminal justice worker if they have one. I would talk to the health visitor and the GP to make sure they know we're involved. A parent could have a history of child care problems with other children in care and you wouldn't know if you didn't talk to other agencies. If workers aren't speaking to each other you don't get the whole picture.

'We work with drug users over a long period of time and it might be that someone goes off the rails and we need to get in touch with other agencies to see if they've had contact. We tell clients that this is the deal, that we have to liaise with appropriate people.' Community psychiatric nurse working in drug service

Responding to child protection concerns

Every agency working with drug users must have a child protection policy which is consistent with local area inter-agency guidelines. All staff should receive training in child protection, ideally jointly with other professionals involved in child protection work.

Drug workers have a duty to contact child protection services if they have concerns about a child's welfare. Potentially, any child living with a parent who misuses drugs may be 'in need' or 'at risk of significant harm'. However, abuse is on a continuum and if every minor incident were reported social services would be overwhelmed. Deciding what constitutes 'significant harm' is a matter of judgement and there are no hard and fast rules. Drug workers are not the right people to make that judgement and decisions about child protection should be made by local area child protection committees. If you are worried about a child, you should seek advice and refer to an appropriate child protection adviser.

If you do not have an in-house child protection adviser, you should try to develop a close working relationship with local children and families social services so that you can discuss concerns informally with an expert. However, you should be aware that social services may decide to conduct an investigation and take the matter out of your hands if they believe a child may be at risk of significant harm.

Child protection procedures

Each local authority or children's services authority has an Area Child Protection Committee (ACPC) with members from children and families social services, police, NSPCC, education, health and other local agencies. The job of the ACPC is to promote and monitor joint child protection policies across all the different agencies and to become involved in individual cases. Every ACPC has a handbook containing detailed guidance on local procedures to be followed in each child protection case.

Under the Children Act 1989 (in England and Wales) the local children's services authority has a duty to make inquiries where they suspect a child in their area is 'suffering, or likely to suffer, significant harm' and to take action to safeguard and promote the child's welfare. Children's services usually convene a child protection conference, bringing together family members and professionals from the relevant agencies to share and evaluate information, make decisions about the risk to the child, and decide whether to instigate proceeding for a care or supervision order. The child protection conference may decide that a child's name should be placed on a child protection register and designate a key worker to take responsibility for their case.

What is 'significant harm'?

Government guidance recommends that when assessing risk of significant harm to a child's development, practitioners consider the degree and extent of physical harm, the duration and frequency of abuse and neglect, the extent to which abuse is premeditated, and the degree of threat, coercion and sadism. Sometimes a single event such as a violent assault or poisoning may constitute significant harm, but more often it is cumulative with a series of events, often over the long term, which damage a child's development. The guidance also states that it is important to consider ill-treatment alongside the family's strengths and supports.

Some drug agencies have a blanket policy of *always* informing social services when a drug using parent with a resident child is attending their service. These are usually agencies working with people with serious drug problems.

> *'We always inform social services when there's a child living with the client. We're not in a position to assess a client's parenting skills or the child. We're upfront about our policy and most people don't have a problem with it. There have been three deaths in the borough where the parent was in treatment, so we have to protect children as well as cover ourselves.'* Nurse working in an inner-city drug team

4

Most agencies contact child protection services only if they have clear grounds for believing that a child may be at risk of significant harm. Professionals providing drug and alcohol counselling services will be concerned that parents will not use their services if they know that they are likely to be reported to social services, rendering them and their children even more vulnerable.

> *'People engage with us because we don't go chatting to other services. We are there to support the client, but we also have to look out for child protection issues. We ask a client about their drug and alcohol use, and get them to talk us through a typical using session. If the client says they drink so much that they fall down and wake up the next day, we would ask them what is happening to the child.*
>
> *'If it became apparent to us that a child was being neglected, we would say to the client that it would be in their best interests for social services to be involved and would try to work with them on it. [Even if the client didn't consent] we would breach confidentiality and contact child protection. But if you disclose against a client's wishes you lose trust and the client will drop out of all contact with services.'* Manager of service providing drug and alcohol counselling for under-25-year-olds

Information databases

The Children Act 2004 introduces new obligations on local children's authorities (in England and Wales) to establish databases for recording and sharing information about individual children. The databases are a response to *Every Child Matters* and Lord Laming's inquiry into the death of Victoria Climbié, which found that poor information sharing between different agencies was a factor contributing to the failure of statutory services to prevent her death. At the time of going to press, the guidance setting out what information should be recorded, who should be required to register information and who would have the power to access it, had not been published. The powers are wide ranging and may have significant implications for agencies working with families affected by drug misuse.

Working with parents who misuse substances: good practice points

- All drug agencies must have clear child protection policies which are consistent with local area child protection procedures. Members of staff should be trained on how to respond to child protection concerns which may arise.

- Every client should be advised of the agency's policies on confidentiality and information sharing early on in their contact with the service. Drug workers should be explicit with clients about the need to break confidentiality if child protection concerns arise.

- Do not assume that people who use drugs are inadequate parents. Parental substance use covers a wide spectrum and should only be a concern where it affects the quality of care a child receives and poses a risk to his/her health or development.

- On the other hand, the potential for harm to all aspects of a child's welfare and development resulting from parental substance use which is heavy, chaotic and illicit cannot be overstated. However much you want to keep a client on board, you cannot sidestep child protection responsibilities. Children have died when professionals have failed to act on concerns.

- Substance misusing parents are often reluctant to use services because they fear their children will be taken away if someone in authority finds out. Like anyone else experiencing difficulties, they are likely to value non-judgemental support rather than criticism.

- If you have concerns about the welfare of a child, unless the situation is an emergency, talk to a designated child protection adviser before contacting child protection services. If you don't have an adviser in your agency, try to establish a good relationship with social services so that you can discuss a case informally. But be aware that if social services decide it is a child protection case they may conduct a formal investigation.

- Unless it would not be in the child's best interest, discuss your concerns with your client and if possible get their consent before making a child protection referral.

- Effective inter-agency working promotes a client's (and their children's) best interests and requires staff working in different agencies to share information on a need to know basis. Always get a client's consent before passing on information unless you are concerned that a child may be at risk of significant harm and it would not be in his/her best interests to do so.

4

Supporting substance misusing parents

Child care law and guidance emphasise the critical role of the family in children's well-being and development. The best outcomes for children are achieved where agencies work in partnership with parents. Partnership working means treating all family members with respect and recognising that family members know more about their family than any professional.

Parents who use/misuse substances usually worry about how this affects their children and how they look after them. Unfortunately, many substance misusing parents have had negative experiences of agencies which have intervened in a policing rather than a supportive role. Parents may feel unable to get support for themselves or their children because they fear they will be judged and criticised rather than supported, or even that their children will be removed. Building a trusting relationship with parents is not always an easy task.

Practical measures for supporting parents

Hidden Harm states that lessening harm to children should be seen as an integral part of drug-related harm reduction and that drug agencies should take on a greater role in promoting children's welfare.

Drug and alcohol workers can help improve children's welfare, without necessarily engaging directly with them, by supporting parents and enhancing their capacity to parent their children effectively. They can do this by:

- offering emotional support and an opportunity to talk about worries

- discussing parenting roles and responsibilities

- building on parents skills and resources

- helping arrange practical support for family

- discussing strategies for managing children's behaviour

- encouraging parents to get involved in activities where they can experience positive role modelling, e.g. if appropriate for the age of the child, by attending local parent and toddler groups

- helping parents to develop routines, guidelines and boundaries with their children

- discussing with parents how they can avoid burdening older children with inappropriate responsibilities

- finding out about and signposting parents to the range of services for children.

Specifically, professionals working with parents who misuse substances can help build protective factors into parenting by *routinely* discussing the following:

- drug safety issues – safe storage of drugs, storage and disposal of injecting equipment, dealing with medical emergencies

- providing for children's basic needs – food, clothes, warmth, hygiene, comfort, security, safety, stimulation, etc

- the importance of a child attending nursery/school, parent and toddler groups, and health appointments with doctor, health visitor, etc

- the protective benefits for a child in developing warm relationships with non-using extended family members and with other families

- issues likely to be harmful for children – e.g. chaotic substance misusing lifestyle, parents using in front of children, children's safety while parents are using or procuring drugs, dealing, and other offending behaviour which may put a child at risk.

Not all drug workers have the experience or training to offer this kind of support to parents. Research evidence indicates that *how* professionals work with parents can be more important than *what* they do. Increasingly, specialist training is available for professionals from different disciplines who work with parents. Drug and alcohol services should allocate someone with specialist training in working with parents to service users who either have a child living with them or have contact with their children.

Early support for a family can prevent difficulties escalating, and subsequent family breakdown. Provision varies between different neighbourhoods, but a range of services for families and children are offered in all parts of the country. Where there are specialist support services available for children of drug and alcohol misusing parents, drug workers may be able to refer families to them without the need for referral to children's/social services.

Parenting education

Parents who misuse substances may lack basic parenting skills. In the last few years, parenting training and education has become increasingly popular with policy makers looking for inexpensive ways of improving children's life chances. Evaluations of parenting education suggest that:

4

- group-based programmes work best because parents benefit from peer support and the opportunity to learn from each other

- programmes should be delivered by trained staff who use empathetic approaches

- programmes should combine practical information about child development and take-home tips for improving behaviour, with cognitive approaches for tackling parents' beliefs and self-perceptions

- parents who have more complex needs or who are experiencing particular difficulties may find one-to-one support more helpful, or may need extra support in using a group-based programme.

Programmes vary enormously, and as with any other kinds of social welfare intervention, however well intentioned they are, there is a potential for harm as well as good. A course led by facilitators who are critical rather than supportive of parents may be counterproductive, undermining parents' confidence and making them reluctant to look for support in future.

Appendix 1: Summary of the main areas of potential impact on health and development of parental problem drug use

(adapted from *Children's needs, parenting capacity: the impact of parental mental illness, problem alcohol and drug use and domestic violence children's development* by Cleaver H. et al. Stationery Office Books, 1999).

Age	Health	Education and cognitive ability	Relationships and identity	Emotional and behavioural development
0–2	Withdrawal syndromes, poor diet and hygiene, routine health checks missed, incomplete immunisation, safety risks due to neglect	Lack of stimulation due to parental preoccupation with drugs and own problems	Problematic attachment to main caregiver, separation from biological parents	Emotional insecurity due to unstable parental behaviour and absences, hyperactivity, inattention, impulsivity and aggression more common

Age	Health	Education and cognitive ability	Relationships and identity	Emotional and behavioural development
3–4	Poor diet, medical and dental checks missed, physical danger due to inadequate supervision, physical violence more common	Lack of stimulation, irregular or no attendance at preschool	Poor attachment to parents, may be required to take excessive responsibility for others	Hyperactivity, inattention, impulsivity, aggression, depression and anxiety more common, fear of separation, inappropriate learned responses due to witnessing violence, theft or adult sex
5–9	School medicals and dental checks missed	Poor school attendance, preparation and concentration due to parental problems and unstable home situation	Restricted friendships, may be required to take on excessive responsibility for parents and siblings	More antisocial acts by boys, depression, anxiety and withdrawal in girls
10–14	Little parental support in puberty, early smoking drinking and drug use more likely	Continued poor academic performance, e.g. if looking after parents or siblings, higher risk of school exclusion	Restricted friendships, poor self-image and low self-esteem	Emotional disturbance, conduct disorders, e.g. bullying, sexual abuse more common, higher risk of offending and criminality
15+	Increased risk of problem alcohol and drug use, pregnancy or sexually transmitted diseases	Lack of educational attainment may affect long-term life chances	Lack of suitable role model	Greater risk of self-blame, guilt, increased suicide risk

4

Appendix 2: Definitions of abuse

(from *Working together to safeguard children: a guide to inter-agency working to safeguard and promote the welfare of children* by Department of Health et al., Stationery Office Books, 1999)

Physical abuse includes hitting, shaking, throwing, poisoning, burning or scalding, drowning or suffocating a child.

Emotional abuse is persistent emotional ill-treatment of a child causing severe and persistent effects on the child's emotional development and may involve:

- conveying to children that they are worthless or unloved, inadequate or valued only in so far as they meet the needs of another person

- imposing developmentally inappropriate expectations

- causing children to feel frightened or in danger – e.g. witnessing domestic violence

- exploitation of corruption of children.

Sexual abuse involves forcing or enticing a child to take part in sexual activities, whether or not they are aware of what is happening. It includes penetrative and non-penetrative acts, and also activities such as involving children in producing or looking at pornography, watching sexual activities or encouraging children to behave in sexually inappropriate ways.

Neglect involves the persistent failure to meet a child's basic physical and/or psychological needs which is likely to result in serious impairment to the child's health and development. It may involve the failure to provide adequate food, shelter or clothing, the failure to protect a child from physical harm or danger or to ensure a child receives appropriate medical care or treatment. It may also include neglect of a child's basic emotional needs.

References

Advisory Council on the Misuse of Drugs (2003) *Hidden Harm*, Home Office

Department Education and Skills *An Overview of Cross Government Guidance: Every Child Matters Change for Children*, 2005 available on line at www.everychildmatters.gov.uk

Scottish Executive (2002) *Getting Our Priorities Right: Good practice guidance for working with children and families affected by substance misuse*

5 | Housing

For people with substance misuse problems, finding and keeping somewhere to live can be a major problem. Drug and alcohol dependency and homelessness are often interconnected, and all too often someone who is going through treatment, with nowhere to live when the programme is finished, ends up using again.

For some clients, simply finding housing is not enough. They may need additional support to be able to make a success of tenancies, such as advice on budgeting, looking after their accommodation or help with getting on with their neighbours or landlord.

This chapter provides basic information about housing provision, law and practice, with the aim of enabling drugs workers to support clients in accessing and keeping housing.

Homelessness

Local authorities' responsibilities towards homeless people with drug and alcohol problems

Councils have no general duty to house people with drug and alcohol problems, however they do have certain legal responsibilities to provide advice and in some cases accommodation to homeless people.

Under Part 7 of the Housing Act 1996 amended by the Housing Act 2002, English and Welsh councils are under a duty to provide/find somewhere to live for people who are **unintentionally homeless and in priority need**.

'Priority need' is a legal definition covering:

- families with children and pregnant women
- people who have been made homeless after a fire, flood or other disaster
- care leavers up to the age of 21
- other people who are vulnerable through old age, mental illness, disability or other special reason.

Homelessness provisions cover not only people having to sleep rough but also people who:

- are likely to be evicted within the next 28 days
- are staying with friends or family in an emergency
- have to move because of violence or threats
- are living in overcrowded conditions

5

- have been locked out of their home

- have nowhere to put their caravan or houseboat

- live in a home which is in such poor repair that it is damaging their health

- are squatting or do not have permission to stay where they are

- whose household is forced to live apart because their accommodation is unsuitable.

If you are advocating for a homeless person who has drug or alcohol problems, you could try to argue that drug and alcohol problems are in themselves a 'special reason'. You could also try referring to case law; for example, in the case of *R v London Borough of Camden ex parte Pereria 1988 'the council had to ask itself whether the applicant was less able to fend for himself/herself when homeless than an ordinary person, or less able to fend for him/herself in finding and keeping accommodation, so that injury or detriment would result to him'*.

Decisions about vulnerability are made on a case-by-case basis. An applicant is more likely to be accepted as 'in priority need' if, in addition to having drug or alcohol problems, they have another vulnerability factor, such as:

- they have been in care, the armed services, prison or other institution

- they are escaping violence or harassment

- they have a disability (including learning disability) or illness

- they are under 25 and have slept on the streets.

'Illness' might include hepatitis B or C, deep vein thrombosis, infected abscesses or mental illness associated with drug use, such as anxiety or depression, for which the client has been referred for therapy or medication. However, councils are unlikely to include everyone who fits into one of these categories, and someone with an illness which is controlled by medication may not be regarded as in priority need.

The local authorities may be persuaded that a client should be accommodated while their priority need is assessed, if their case is supported by a letter from a drug worker or other agency.

Procedure for making a homelessness application

Some local authorities have a specific office that deals with homelessness applications, but others may operate several offices in different parts of their area or delegate the responsibility to a housing association. The local authority switchboard should be able to provide advice on which office a client should approach to make a homelessness application. Most local authorities expect people to go in person to make an application, and to attend an interview. If someone becomes homeless outside office hours, there should be an out-of-hours service that can be contacted.

A client must make a homelessness application within 28 days if they are already homeless or are threatened with homelessness, e.g. because they are leaving an institution or have to leave their accommodation. They should take any evidence with them that will help to back up their application, for example:

- identification such as birth certificates or passports for everyone in their household

- proof of income (e.g. benefit book or wage slips)

- child benefit book

- proof of pregnancy

- tenancy agreement

- eviction notice served by landlord

- court possession papers

- a letter from the person who has asked them to leave

- a letter saying when they will be discharged from an institution.

Local connection rules

A local authority should not refuse to consider an application because it is deemed the person does not have a local connection, but it may decide to refer them to another authority. To establish a local connection someone has to show, for example, that they:

- have lived in the area for six months out of the past 12 (being in prison or hospital in the area may not count), or

- have close family who have lived in the area for at least five years, or

- works in the area.

These rules should not apply to someone who has fled their local area because of violence or threats of violence.

5

Applicants from abroad

People without British citizenship or who have lived abroad recently may not be entitled to assistance even if they meet the other criteria. They should seek advice from a specialist adviser.

The local authority's decision

The local authority will write to the applicant informing them of its decision. If it is decided that the applicant is not eligible to be provided with accommodation the council should explain the reasons.

If the local authority finds that the applicant is unintentionally homeless and in priority need, it has to find accommodation for the applicant for two years. This could be a house or flat or a place in a hostel or bed and breakfast hotel. Families with children should not be placed in private bed and breakfast or hostel accommodation which is not self-contained.

If the applicant turns down the accommodation offered, the local authority does not have to find anything else. However, the applicant can appeal if they thinks the offer is unsuitable.

Priority need

The local authority may decide that an applicant is homeless but does not meet the criteria for priority need, in which case it has no legal responsibility to house the person. Some authorities may agree to house the applicant anyway if it accepts that they are unintentionally homeless. However, in parts of the country where pressures on housing are acute, the person is likely to be asked to leave emergency accommodation if it has been provided by the council.

The applicant is entitled to ask the council to review the decision by appealing in writing within 21 days of receipt of the decision letter.

'Intentionally homeless'

The local authority may deem an applicant to be 'intentionally homeless', for example because they were evicted from their previous accommodation for antisocial behaviour or for not paying the rent, or because they left of their own accord.

Under section 196(1) of the Housing Act 1996, *'A person becomes threatened with homelessness intentionally if he deliberately does or fails to do anything the likely result of which is that he will be forced to leave accommodation which is available for his occupation and which it would have been reasonable for him to continue to occupy...'*

If the client believes the council is wrong – e.g. if they left their home because of violence or they were evicted because they could not afford to pay the rent – they can ask for the decision to be reviewed.

If the council decides that an applicant is intentionally homeless, it has no legal obligation to provide housing for them. However, if the person is deemed to be 'in priority need', the council should still provide them with emergency accommodation for up to 28 days to give them time to make other arrangements.

Help from social services

Some people who apply to the housing department for help are referred to social services. This may be because the housing department thinks they are especially vulnerable and so need particular help with housing (e.g. because of disability or a mental health problem), or because they fall outside the criteria for help under homelessness legislation but may be entitled to help because of their vulnerability.

Social services may have a duty to find emergency accommodation for someone who is homeless or about to become homeless if they:

- are aged 16 or 17 years old
- are leaving (or have left) care
- are elderly
- have physical or mental health problems
- are disabled.

In the longer term, they may help with finding accommodation, which could include:

- getting a council or housing association home
- paying the deposit for a private sector tenancy
- getting a place in specialist housing.

Social services have a duty to house children even if the family is deemed to be intentionally homeless. Under the Children Act, social services are supposed to try to keep families together, although they may try to offer accommodation for children only.

Social services and housing departments should work together to provide services. Unfortunately this does not always happen. Getting through to the right person may require some persistence.

Care leavers

Young people aged up to 21 who have been in care are entitled to help with housing.

Care leavers aged 16 or 17 remain the responsibility of the social services department that last looked after them, even if they move to another area. The department is responsible for providing suitable accommodation, which could be in a children's home, hostel, foyer, bed and breakfast hotel or flat, and for supporting them financially by paying for food, bills, travel, clothing, etc.

Homeless care leavers aged 18 to 21 are automatically classed as in priority need and are entitled to help from both housing and social services departments.

People aged over 21 who have been in care may also be able to show that they are in priority need, e.g. if they have slept rough or not had a stable home since leaving care.

Emergency accommodation

If someone has nowhere to stay one night or is about to be discharged from an institution with nowhere to go, they may be able to get a place at an emergency hostel, night shelter or bed and breakfast hotel.

Hostels and night shelters sometimes accept people who turn up at the door, provided they have space. However, in some areas there may be a waiting list, or only people referred by the council or another agency are accepted. The hostel or night shelter may be willing to accept a referral from a drug worker, but not a self-referral.

Some emergency accommodation is reserved for particular groups such as young people, people with drug or alcohol problems, or people with mental health problems, and may offer additional support. Again, a referral from a drug worker may help a client access this kind of accommodation.

Hostels and night shelters generally ban alcohol as well as street drugs and may be unwilling to admit people who arrive obviously drunk or drugged. Clients need to be aware that such accommodation usually enforces rules strictly and that if they break them they are likely to be evicted and may find it difficult to get accepted in other emergency housing.

Night shelters

These are usually very basic and just provide a place to stay for a few nights and usually a meal. Many night shelters are open only during the winter and may be based in disused churches and offices. Most are free.

Hostels

Hostels rarely accept couples, and residents may have to share a room as well as other facilities. Some hostels allow people to stay for a few months and help them to find longer-term or move-on accommodation before they leave.

The rent charged by a hostel may not be fully covered by housing benefit. Housing benefit does not cover extras meals or cleaning. Clients need to be prepared to meet some of the cost out of wages or welfare benefits such as income support.

Bed and breakfast hotels

These are usually more expensive than hostels and they may charge rent in advance. They may be privately owned and run, or they may belong to a local authority. Most of the cheaper bed and breakfast hotels have shared bathrooms and no cooking facilities, and residents may not be allowed to stay in the hotel during the day. Not all will accept homeless people, young people under 18 or people on housing benefit. Residents can be evicted very easily if they fail to pay rent, even if this is due to delays in receiving housing benefit.

Longer-term accommodation

Foyers

Foyers offer hostel-style accommodation for disadvantaged young people up to the age of about 25. They aim to provide a bridge to independence by integrating training, job search and personal support with a place to live. Foyers work closely with the local careers service, training agencies and employers, and residents are expected to sign up for a training course, education programme or apprenticeship.

Most foyers are purpose built, housing 100 or more young people, but some are smaller converted houses. Foyers are independent and have been funded in a variety of ways, for example through partnerships between housing associations and local colleges, and many have received regeneration funding. They generally offer a higher standard of accommodation than hostels and provide meals and other services like cleaning. Residents can usually stay for nine months to a year and foyer staff will generally help them to find affordable accommodation to move into afterwards.

Foyers usually have a waiting list, and although some accept self-referrals prospective residents may need to be referred by the council, an emergency hostel or other agency. Residents are usually interviewed and required to sign an agreement that they will comply with foyer rules and participate in education and training opportunities.

Residents on a low income can claim housing benefit; however, this may not cover the full rent and they will have to meet the cost of meals and cleaning from their own income. People who cause a nuisance to other residents or who do not pay the rent or follow their training programme are likely to be evicted.

Information about local foyers can be obtained from the council, local Learning and Skills Council, or the Foyer Federation website at www.foyer.net/mn/

Supported housing

Local authorities, housing associations and voluntary organisations provide supported housing for vulnerable people. Each provider sets its own rules for allocating accommodation and sometimes people with drug or alcohol problems will only be considered if, for example, they are disabled or have a severe mental health problem.

Supported housing can be a good option for people who have been through detox or rehab and are motivated to get their drug use under control, but are not yet able to cope with their own tenancy and need help with day-to-day living. Some supported housing units are aimed specifically at people with substance misuse problems but units which are targeted at other groups – e.g. older people, people with mental health problems or people from particular religious or cultural backgrounds – may be more suitable for some clients. The level and type of support provided varies widely, from 24-hour support to occasional advice on budgeting, welfare benefits, cooking and so on. Rent levels vary considerably and may not always be covered fully by housing benefit.

There is often a waiting list for supported housing and providers may interview prospective residents before accepting them. It may be possible to arrange for a client to go straight into supported housing after being discharged from treatment, but this kind of specialist housing is in short supply and rarely available at short notice.

Supporting People

Supporting People is the government programme which funds low-level housing-related support services for vulnerable people in England, including those with substance abuse problems. The programme is aimed at preventing people becoming homeless or being moved into more expensive care, and covers both supported housing units and floating support for those living in their own tenancies or their own homes. It is intended to be flexible in terms of both the level and intensity of provision.

Every local authority should have a nominated Supporting People team who work with drug action teams and other local drug services to commission services.

Further information about Supporting People, including local authority contacts, is available on the Office for the Deputy Prime Minister website at www.spkweb.org.uk

Tenancy support and resettlement services

Most local authorities provide some form of tenancy and/or resettlement support for vulnerable people. The kind of services offered range from personal support to help with removals and getting second-hand furniture, to advice on budgeting and accessing benefits. Intensive support may be available for vulnerable people leaving an institution or moving from supported housing into their own tenancy, with the intensity and level of support tapering off as they become more independent. In some areas, these services may be available for anyone with a history of substance misuse but elsewhere it may be targeted at those with an additional vulnerability – e.g. young people or those with dual diagnosis or a disability. Again, a letter of referral from a drug worker may help a client to access services.

Council and housing association tenancies

For a client who is looking for long-term housing, council and housing association properties are attractive options, but in practice they can be very hard to come by. It is also worth bearing in mind that they may not be the right option for someone whose drug use and lifestyle is chaotic. If they are evicted for failing to pay the rent, they may forfeit their entitlement to a tenancy in the future.

Local authority and housing association tenancies are cheaper than comparable private sector housing and generally offer tenants much better rights. Tenants cannot usually be evicted without good cause and so a tenancy can be for life. However, waiting lists are usually long and the only available accommodation may be on large estates or in tower blocks. Even families with children and others with high priority needs may have to wait a long time. In some areas, there may be little prospect of single people ever getting a tenancy because other applicants have higher priority.

How to apply

A client wishing to apply for a council or housing association flat or house should contact the local authority and ask for an application form, and also ask local housing associations whether they have separate waiting lists. Tenancies are assigned to people on the housing register (waiting list) according to local allocation policies and applicants' circumstances, including the suitability of their present housing.

5

Who is eligible

A council may refuse to place an applicant on the waiting list if, for example, they have recently arrived from abroad or if they have no local connection with the area. Former tenants with debts from a previous tenancy or who have been found guilty of antisocial behaviour are also likely to be excluded.

Secure or assured tenancies

Most housing associations, local authorities and housing action trusts offer either a secure tenancy or an assured tenancy. These agreements give tenants the right to stay in the accommodation as long as they keep to the terms of the tenancy agreement. However, if the tenancy agreement is broken, for example, because of rent arrears or nuisance to neighbours, the landlord can serve a notice on the tenant and apply to the county court for eviction. If this happens, the tenant should consult an experienced adviser.

Introductory tenancies

Some local authorities and social landlords make all new tenants introductory tenants for the first 12 months of the tenancy, giving them some but not all of the rights of secure tenants. At the end of this period the tenancy is normally converted to a secure tenancy, providing the tenant has complied with the terms of the agreement.

It is very easy for a landlord to evict an introductory tenant – for example, for causing a nuisance to neighbours or failing to pay rent regularly.

Private rented accommodation

Rising housing costs and high demand for social housing in many parts of the country mean that, particularly for single people and couples without children, the only realistic option for getting a place they can call home may be through the private rented sector.

Points for prospective tenants to bear in mind

- Letting agents can be a good source of information about local properties but clients need to be aware they act on behalf of landlords, not tenants and it is illegal for them to charge for giving out lists of accommodation or for putting people on their books.

- For their own safety, it's a good idea if a client takes someone with them when they go to view a property.

- Housing benefit may not cover the full rent for a property (see below).

- Many landlords will not accept people on housing benefit.

- Many landlords require people to give references before they will accept them as tenants.

- Young people may be asked for a guarantor for the rent.

- Contracts can be legalistic and difficult to understand. Once signed they are legally binding, so clients may need advice to ensure they understand the implications fully before they sign.

Assured shorthold tenancies

Most private tenants nowadays have assured shorthold tenancies. This means they have a right to occupy the property for the period specified in the tenancy agreement (a minimum of six months). Often, they are able to renew the agreement for another specified period. However, after the term of the agreement has expired the landlord can apply to courts for repossession if they wish, provided they have given the tenants at least two months' notice.

Other rights of assured shorthold tenants include:

- the right to have the property maintained in a reasonable state of repair

- the right for the tenant to carry out minor repairs themselves and to deduct the cost from the rent

- the right for the tenant's partner of the opposite sex to take over the tenancy if they die

- the right to stay in the property for the period of the tenancy unless the landlord has the tenant evicted by a court, e.g. for rent arrears, damaging the property or breaking the terms of the agreement.

Landlords cannot normally increase the rent during the period of the contract unless the tenant agrees or the tenancy agreement permits this.

Repairs

Landlords are legally responsible for keeping the property in reasonable repair. This covers:

5

- the structure and outside of the property, including the roof, drains, pipes and gutters

- water and gas pipes, electrical wiring, plumbing, sinks, baths and toilets

- gas fires and other fixed heaters and water heaters (but not cookers)

- repairs to parts of the building, such as stairways and hallways, shared with the landlord or other tenants.

If the landlord wants to carry out repairs or improvements, they must either get the tenant's permission to enter the home and do the work, or get a court order authorising them to take possession of the home. If the repairs are so extensive that they cannot be done without the tenant moving out, the landlord may have to provide the tenant with alternative accommodation.

Right to repair

Local authority and housing association tenants may be able to use 'right to repair' schemes to claim compensation for repairs affecting their health, safety or security which the landlord does not carry out within a set timescale. Tenants should apply to the landlord for details of such schemes.

Safety of electrical and gas appliances

Landlords are responsible for ensuring that any gas or electrical appliances such as heaters, cookers and kettles supplied with the accommodation are safe. The landlord must arrange and pay for safety checks and any necessary work to be carried out on gas appliances at least once every 12 months.

Wear and tear and damage

Most household furniture and contents deteriorate, and landlords are responsible for repairing or replacing items which break down or become dangerously worn through normal wear and tear, unless this is due to negligence on behalf of the tenant.

Tenants are required to take reasonable care of the property, including being responsible for internal decoration and doing little jobs like unblocking drains. They are also required to pay for damage to the property or to furniture or other contents supplied with the accommodation. The cost of replacement or repairs may be deducted from the deposit at the end of the tenancy or the landlord might take legal action for compensation.

Lodgers and sub-tenants

Private tenants do not have the right to take in lodgers or sub-tenants without the landlord's agreement, unless this is specified in the tenancy agreement. Local authority and housing association tenants can usually take in lodgers (who are provided with meals or other services), but need to get the landlord's permission before sub-letting all or part of the property (even one room). Unauthorised sub-letting may give the landlord grounds to evict.

Harassment by the landlord

It is an offence for a landlord to do anything which they know is likely to make a tenant leave the property or to prevent the tenant from exercising their legal rights. This might include repeatedly disturbing tenants late at night or obstructing access to the property, creating noise, or disconnecting water, gas or electricity supplies.

A tenant who is being harassed by their landlord should contact the Tenancy Relations Officer of the local authority or the police.

Housing and antisocial behaviour

Since the introduction of the Antisocial Behaviour Act 2003, the law against antisocial behaviour has become much tougher. Antisocial behaviour includes:

- intimidation or harassment of neighbours, including racial harassment
- verbal abuse, including homophobic abuse
- drug dealing
- noise
- vandalism
- dumping rubbish
- animal rubbish
- any conduct which may cause a nuisance or annoyance.

A client who is unhappy about a neighbour's antisocial behaviour may be able to take action themselves, for example by contacting a tenants' association (if there is one), seeking mediation or asking to be rehoused themselves (e.g. if they live in housing owned by a local authority or a social landlord). Alternatively, they can try to get the landlord, local authority or police to deal with the behaviour.

5

If the person behaving in an antisocial manner is a tenant, they may be in breach of their tenancy agreement and so the landlord may be able to evict them. Under Part 2 of the Antisocial Behaviour Act 2003, local authorities (and housing action trusts and other social landlords) also have a range of powers for dealing with antisocial behaviour:

- applying for a court order to stop the behaviour (this may include prohibiting someone from being in a particular building or area)

- evicting the person responsible if they are a local authority tenant

- offering the victim alternative accommodation

- prosecuting the perpetrator if the behaviour is a criminal offence.

In certain cases, for example if violence or threats of violence are involved, someone who fails to comply with the terms of a court order may be arrested.

Clients should be aware that if they behave in an antisocial manner themselves, they may face an on-the-spot fine, be liable to prosecution or face eviction from their property (even if they have a secure tenancy).

Housing, drugs and criminal law

Particularly in accommodation such as hostels, foyers and supported housing, owners and managers are generally very strict about enforcing 'no drugs' rules. Police operations can be mounted on any residential setting at any time and managers can be prosecuted under the Misuse of Drugs Act 1971 for knowingly allowing their premises to be used for producing or selling any illegal drug, or for the taking of certain drugs.

Tenants living in rented accommodation may be evicted for drug use if their tenancy agreement forbids them from engaging in illegal activity or if there is antisocial behaviour associated with the drug use (see above).

Closure notices and closure orders

- Under Part 1 of the Antisocial Behaviour Act 2003, the police can put a **closure notice** on a building if they have reasonable grounds for believing that it is being used in connection with the **use, production or supply of a Class A drug** and if there has been a serious nuisance to the public. Anyone who then tries to enter the building who does not live there can be arrested.

  The most commonly used Class A drugs include cocaine, crack cocaine, heroin and other opiates and ecstasy.

'Serious nuisance' is not defined by statute, but Home Office guidance suggests it may include:

- intimidating and threatening behaviour towards residents
- a significant increase in crime in the immediate area surrounding the accommodation
- sexual acts being committed in public
- consistent need to collect and dispose of drugs paraphernalia and other dangerous items
- high numbers of people entering and leaving the premises over a 24-hour period and the resultant disruption they cause to residents
- noise – constant/intrusive noise – excessive noise at all hours associated with visitors to the property.

Within 48 hours of the closure notice being issued, the police can apply to the courts for a **closure order** to be put on the building. If the court agrees to the order, the building must be closed and anyone who tries to enter can be arrested, even if they live there. The police can claim costs associated with clearing, securing or maintaining the building from the owner.

There is a right of appeal against the closure order for people who have an interest in the building, and someone who suffers financial loss as a result of the order but who is not connected with the illegal drug-related activity is entitled to claim compensation.

Squatting

Squatting in an empty property is not illegal. However, it is a criminal offence to get into a property by breaking in or damaging windows and doors, and squatters can be arrested even if the damage is minimal. Squatters can be evicted very easily and may be arrested if they refuse to leave when the landlord gets a court order, or the person who normally lives in the property or has a right to move in asks them to leave. It is also illegal for squatters to use services such as gas, electricity or water without contacting the supplier first.

Squatters are classed as homeless because they do not have a legal right to live in the property and so may be eligible for assistance from the local authority.

For more information about squatting, visit the website of the Advisory Service for Squatters at www.squatter.org.uk or telephone 020 7359 8814 or 0845 644 5814.

5

Housing-related welfare benefits and other financial help with housing

Housing benefit

Tenants on a low income may be entitled to housing benefit to cover all or part of their rent. Housing benefit does not cover other services, such as meals or cleaning, which may be provided at the accommodation.

Entitlement to housing benefit is assessed according to the applicant's income (whether from work or benefits), level of savings, the area in which they live, their age and the number of people living with them. Single people under 25 are expected to live in a bedsit, but people over the age of 25 can claim for a one-bedroom flat. In order to set the amount of rent on which housing benefit can be paid, the housing benefit officer will compare the rent the claimant is paying with rents for similar properties locally. If they think the property is too expensive, they will only agree to pay part of the rent.

Housing benefit rules are complicated, so a client may wish to ask the housing benefit office for a pre-tenancy determination before they sign a contract for a property. This will prevent them committing to a property they cannot afford.

Social fund loans

People on very low incomes without savings can apply to the local Jobcentre Plus or the Department for Work and Pensions (DWP) office for a social fund loan to help them pay rent in advance. A limited amount of money is available from the social fund and the chances of getting a loan depend on individual circumstances. A letter from a drug worker may help persuade the DWP that a particular client should be a priority. However, loans have to be repaid within 78 weeks and an applicant will not receive a loan if they cannot afford to repay it.

Further information about social fund loans is available from the Citizens Advice Bureau website at: www.nacab.org.uk

Deposit guarantee schemes

Most private landlords require at least one month's rent in advance plus one month's rent as a deposit. People who lack the resources to pay the deposit may be able to join a deposit guarantee scheme run by a local authority, housing association or voluntary organisation. Schemes vary but usually no money exchanges hands at the beginning of the tenancy and the scheme will guarantee to pay the landlord for any damage which may occur. At the end of the tenancy, the tenant is required to reimburse the scheme.

Help with home improvements and adaptations

Local authorities run schemes to help people on low incomes with the cost of repairs and adaptations to their home. Generally, landlords are responsible for maintaining privately rented housing, but it may be worthwhile for a client to contact the local authority to see if it can help with the cost of improvements, including the installation of central heating or insulation, or adaptations for a disabled person. A tenant must get the landlord's agreement before any improvements or adaptations are carried out.

Useful websites

Further information on the issues covered in this chapter are available from **Shelter**. Shelter provides a national telephone advice line staffed by trained housing advisers. You can ring on Freephone **0808 800 4444** seven days a week from 8am to midnight. Online information available at www.shelter.org.uk/advice/index.cfm which includes a directory of local housing advice services.

The **National Housing Federation** website www.housing.org.uk lists supported housing providers, with links for local contacts.

The **Office for the Deputy Prime Minister** website provides information on local contacts for Supporting People: www.spkweb.org.uk

Citizens Advice Bureau website: www.nacab.org.uk

6 Welfare rights

This chapter provides basic information about welfare benefits that clients may be eligible to claim.

Jobseeker's allowance (JSA)

JSA is a benefit for people who are unemployed and looking for work. There are two kinds of JSA, contribution-based and income-based.

To receive either contribution-based or income-based JSA the claimant needs to be available for work immediately and 'actively seeking work'. They may be asked to provide evidence that they are making real efforts to find a job, for example letters of application or rejection letters from an employer. Claimants who are not available for work due to illness may be able to claim incapacity benefit (see below).

JSA is paid at different rates according to the applicant's age. People **over 25** get a higher rate. Claimants **under the age of 18** who are not in education or employment may be entitled to JSA provided they have not been offered a place on a government training scheme, and should consult an experienced adviser.

Contribution-based JSA

This is for unemployed people who have been in work long enough in the previous two years to have paid sufficient national insurance contributions. A claimant is entitled to contribution-based JSA even if they have savings or a partner is working, provided they have an adequate contributions record. Contribution-based JSA is paid for a maximum of six months.

Income-based JSA

This is a benefit for unemployed people who have not paid enough national insurance contributions to receive contribution-based JSA, or for whom contribution-based JSA would not be enough to live on, for example because they have a partner. Entitlement to income-based JSA depends on a person's income and capital (savings or property). Applicants for income-based JSA usually have to make a joint application with their partner, and both of them have to meet the conditions for looking for work. People who work part time may be entitled to receive income-based JSA, depending on their income and the number of hours they work.

People claiming income-based JSA who have children living with them need to make a separate claim for child tax credit using a form from HM Revenue and Customs (HMRC).

6

To make an application for JSA

Claimants can either go to the local Jobcentre Plus or the Department of Work and Pensions (DWP) office, or can telephone the office and ask for an application form to be sent to them. An officer will help them fill in the form if they need it. They will then have to attend an interview. If their application is successful they will have to return to the office to sign on at a specified time and day – usually every two weeks.

Sanctions

A claimant who left their previous job voluntarily or who was sacked for misconduct may be sanctioned, which could mean waiting for up to six months before they are entitled to receive jobseeker's allowance. If there were good reasons for leaving a job, the decision can be challenged and the claimant should seek advice.

If the DWP/Jobcentre Plus thinks the claimant is not doing enough to find work, they may make a direction requiring them, for example, to attend an interview or course or to apply for a job. If the claimant fails to follow the direction, they may be sanctioned and have their benefit cut. Similarly, if they turn down a job offer without good reason they may be sanctioned.

Disagreement with a JSA decision

If a claimant disagrees with a decision about JSA they can ask for the decision to be reviewed or appeal against the decision. There are strict time limits for these.

Further information about the review of benefit decisions and rights of appeal is contained in the DWP leaflet *If you think our decision is wrong*

available from local social security offices or the DWP website at www.dwp.gov.uk/publications/dwp/2003/gl24_apr.pdf

Hardship payments

A claimant who is sanctioned and does not have enough money to live on may be able to claim a discretionary hardship payment. As with other discretionary payments, a letter from a drug worker or other agency working with the claimant providing evidence of the risk of hardship may increase their chances of being successful.

Income support (IS)

Income support is a benefit for people with no alternative source of income or very low income with limited savings who are not required to look for work, for example because they are bringing up children alone or because they are sick, disabled or a carer.

Applying for IS

To make an application for IS the claimant should go to the local DWP or Jobcentre Plus office. If they have children living with them they will have to make a separate claim for child tax credit from HMRC.

Unable to work due to illness or disability

People who are unable to work because of illness or disability (which could be linked to drug problems) should get a medical certificate from their doctor before going to the DWP or Jobcentre Plus office to make their claim for IS. They are required to pass a **personal capability assessment**.

The personal capability assessment is a detailed questionnaire about what the claimant can and cannot do. The DWP will send them the questionnaire to fill in and will then decide whether they think the claimant is capable of work. They may require the claimant to be assessed in person by a benefits agency doctor.

Appeals

If the claimant does not agree with the decision about income support they can appeal.

Incapacity benefit

Incapacity benefit (IB) is for people who are unable to work because of sickness or disability who have paid sufficient national insurance contributions and who are not entitled to statutory sick pay from an employer.

Rates of benefit

Incapacity benefit is paid at different levels according to how long a person has been sick. Additional money may be paid for an adult dependant. For the first 28 weeks, the claimant may be entitled to lower rate short-term IB and will usually have to provide evidence that they are incapable of work by sending in medical certificates from their doctor. They may also be required to attend an interview.

After 28 weeks, the claimant should receive a higher rate of benefit. At some point during their claim they will have to pass the personal capability assessment. This involves a detailed questionnaire that looks at the claimant's ability to perform a range of specified activities and may include a medical examination.

Long-term IB is paid after a year of sickness. Additional money can be paid according to the claimant's age and for an adult dependant and children.

6

Contribution conditions

If a claimant is unsure whether they meet the contribution conditions, for example because they have not been working for all of the previous two years, or if their income is low, it is advisable to claim income support (IS) at the same time as incapacity benefit. They may be able to get IS instead of, or as well as, IB. Information about national insurance contributions is available at the NACAB website at: www.adviceguide.org.uk/ index/life/benefits/national_insurance_contributions_and_contributory_benefits.htm

To claim incapacity benefit

The claimant should complete a self-certificate form SC1, available from local benefit offices, GP surgeries and hospitals or online at the DWP website, and send it to the local DWP office. After the first week of sickness, the claimant needs to get a medical certificate from their GP and complete an IB form and, if necessary, an IS claim form.

Housing benefit

Claimants receiving IS or means-tested JSA who are paying rent as a tenant or lodger or who are living in a hostel are entitled to receive housing benefit. They should receive an application form for housing benefit from the DWP or Jobcentre Plus office when they claim JSA or IS. Other people on low incomes with limited savings may also be entitled to housing benefit and should apply at the local housing benefit office.

What it covers

Housing benefit can only be paid for the rent for the accommodation and for charges for services such as a caretaker, communal laundry facilities and play areas. In Northern Ireland it also covers rate rebates.

Housing benefit does **not** cover:

- mortgage payments. People on IS, income-based JSA or pension credit may be able to get help with these payments

- water charges

- charges for heating, hot water, lighting, cooking which are sometimes included in the rent

- payments for food or fuel in board and lodgings or hostels.

Entitlement to housing benefit

This is based on an applicant's (and their partner's) income, savings, the area in which they live, their age and who else is living with them. In order to set the amount of rent on which housing benefit can be paid, the rent officer will compare the rent the claimant is paying with rents for similar properties locally. If they think the property is too expensive they will only agree to pay part of the rent.

There are also rules about the size of accommodation people are entitled to claim for. For example, single people under 25 are expected to live in a bedsit while those over 25 can claim for a one-bedroom flat. **Clients should not assume that all their rent will be covered by housing benefit.**

Pre-tenancy determinations

To avoid committing themselves to a property they cannot afford, it may be a good idea for clients to ask the housing benefit office for a pre-tenancy determination before they sign any contract.

Right of appeal

Clients who disagree with the housing benefit department's decision have a right of appeal. Strict time limits apply.

Council tax benefits

Claimants receiving IS or means-tested JSA are entitled to receive council tax benefit and should receive an application form along with their application for JSA or IS. Other people on a low income may also entitled be council tax benefit and should apply directly to the housing benefit office local authority.

Second adult rebates

Households with only one adult are entitled to a 25% reduction in their council tax bill and should apply to the local authority. If a claimant is not entitled to council tax benefit but there is a second adult in the property on a low income, the claimant may be entitled to a second adult rebate.

Social fund loans

The social fund is intended to help people in need with certain important expenses. Applications to the social fund are decided upon in different ways, depending on the type

6

of payment. Some payments, such as maternity grants and funeral payments, are based on the applicant meeting the conditions of entitlement. Community care grants and crisis loans are discretionary and depend on the local DWP's assessment of the claimant's priority of need. For these payments, the support of a drug worker or other agency verifying the claimant's vulnerability can make the difference between success and failure of the application.

Community care grants

Community care grants from the social fund are for people on low incomes who need extra financial help to enable them to live independently. Only people receiving income support or income-based JSA, or who are eligible for one of these when they leave residential care or an institution, are entitled to apply.

Community care grants are discretionary and the budget is limited. Only people in difficult circumstances are usually able to get them. However, it is worth a client applying if, for example:

- they are leaving residential care or an institution
- they have not had a stable home for a long time (e.g. if they have been sleeping on the streets)
- their family is under extreme pressure (e.g. because of a long-term illness, separation or divorce)
- they are looking after someone who is disabled, ill, or a prisoner or young offender on home leave.

Community care grants can be used to cover costs, such as:

- furniture, bedding and household equipment
- connection charges for gas and electricity
- clothing and shoes
- removal expenses
- essential travel expenses (e.g. to go to a funeral or visit their children or someone who is ill).

Community care grants cannot be used for rent in advance nor for a whole host of other expenses, from sports clothing and school uniform to the costs of a telephone. Other excluded items are listed on the NACAB website.

Clients can get an application form at the local DWP office or Jobcentre Plus. Because it is not easy to get a payment they may need help in filling in the application. A letter from a drug worker or other adviser verifying their vulnerability may make all the difference to their chances.

If a community care grant is refused or the applicant receives less than the amount they applied for, they can ask the DWP (Social Security Agency in Northern Ireland) to review the decision. If they are still unhappy with the outcome, they can ask for an independent review by the Independent Review Service for the Social Fund (IRS). The IRS review is quick and easy, and routine cases are dealt with within 12 days. The IRS regularly change more than half of the community care grants decisions that it reviews.

For further information about the IRS go to www.irs-review.org.uk

Crisis loans

Crisis loans are interest-free loans intended to help people with limited means deal with an emergency. A crisis loan can be paid for any specific need (providing it is not excluded) to meet expenses in an emergency, or as a consequence of a disaster. The crisis loan must provide help which is the only means by which serious damage or risk to the health or safety of the claimant or their family can be avoided.

Crisis loans can also be used to pay rent in advance to avoid damage or risk to health or safety in an emergency or disaster. If the claimant has been awarded a community care grant to help them set up home after a period of homelessness or time in an institution they are generally able to get a crisis loan to pay for rent advance.

The chances of a claimant receiving a crisis loan and the amount of the loan are dependent on personal circumstances. As with other social fund payments, a claimant may be more likely to be successful if they get help with their application and have evidence (for example, a letter from a drugs worker) of their vulnerability.

Applications for crisis loans can be made in person at the local DWP or Jobcentre Plus office, or by completing an application form. These offices have to accept the application and not just tell someone they are not eligible without giving them an application form or interviewing them.

Claimants have to pay back the loan within 78 weeks. If they are on benefits, a fixed amount will be taken out of their IS or JSA until the loan has been repaid. People who cannot afford to repay a loan are unlikely to be awarded one.

If a crisis loan is refused, or the claimant is awarded less than they applied for, they can ask for a review of the decision. If they are still unhappy with the outcome they have the right to ask for an independent review by the IRS. Urgent crisis loan reviews are handled within 24 hours.

Budgeting loans

A budgeting loan is an interest-free loan from the social fund intended to help people who have been on IS or JSA for more than six months spread the cost of occasional expenses such as:

- furniture and household equipment

- clothing and shoes

- travel expenses

- rent in advance and/or removal expenses if you have to move home

- essential home improvements, maintenance or security

- expenses related to finding a job (a suit, for example).

Applicants may also be able to take out a loan to pay off hire purchase or other debts incurred to buy items like those listed above.

The minimum amount which can be awarded is £30 and the maximum is £1,000. To get a budgeting loan, the applicant or their partner must have been on IS, income-based JSA or pension credit for at least 26 weeks. The budget for social fund loans is cash limited and the chances of an applicant getting a loan and how much will depend on personal circumstances, including:

- how long they have been on benefits

- the number of people in their household

- their savings

- whether they already owe money to the social fund because of a previous loan.

Applications for budgeting loans should be submitted to the local DWP or Jobcentre Plus office. Before making an application it is worth the client checking whether they might be entitled to a community care grant, maternity grant or funeral payment, which do not have to be repaid. Clients are likely to need help making an application to convince the DWP or Jobcentre Plus that they should be a priority.

Budgeting loans normally have to be paid back in full within 78 weeks. If the applicant is on benefits, a fixed sum is deducted from their income support or jobseeker's allowance until the loan has been repaid. If the DWP believe the applicants won't be able to afford to repay a loan they won't get one.

If a budgeting loan is refused, or the applicant is awarded less than they applied for, they can ask for a review of the decision. If they are still unhappy with the outcome, they have the right to ask for an independent review by the IRS. There are strict time limits for reviews.

Other welfare benefits clients may be able to claim

Child tax credit (CTC)

This is a means-tested benefit for people bringing up children whose income is below around £50,000 a year. The amount of child tax credit payable depends on the number and ages of the children and on parents' income. A higher rate is payable for disabled children getting disability living allowance.

Working tax credit (WTC)

People who are working and whose income is modest may be able to get extra money. The rules about entitlement are complicated, and depend on age, how many hours the claimant is working, whether they have a disability or have dependent children.

Applying for CTC or WTC

Further information and application details for both child tax credit and working tax credit is available at the HM Revenue and Customs (HMRC) website: www.taxcredits.inlandrevenue.gov.uk or the tax credit helpline: 0845 300 3900 (Textphone 0845 300 3909)

Application packs for working tax credit and child tax credit are also available from HMRC Enquiry Centres, local social security offices, job centres and Jobcentre Plus offices.

Child benefit

Child benefit can be paid to any person who is bringing up children. There is a fixed amount for each child and it is not affected by the claimant's income or savings.

Disability living allowance (DLA)

This is for people who need help with care or mobility needs because of a physical or mental illness or disability. Disability living allowance can also be paid for a child with a disability who has care and/or mobility needs.

Carer's allowance

This is a means-tested benefit for people who spend at least 35 hours a week caring for a person with a disability who is receiving certain benefits. Carers may also be able to claim IS.

Maternity grant

This is intended to help people on a low income (e.g. on IS or income-based JSA) buy clothes and equipment for a baby. It can be claimed by a pregnant woman (or her partner) within three months of the birth or adoption of a child. The grant does not have to be repaid and is currently worth £500.

Funeral payment

This is intended to help with the cost of essential funeral expenses for people on low incomes. People on IS, income-based JSA, pension credit, housing benefit or council tax benefit may be able to claim a funeral payment following the death of a partner or a child, or the death of another member of the family if no other immediate relative has the means to pay.

Pensions and welfare benefits for older people

Women aged 60 or over and men aged 65 or over may be entitled to a state retirement pension, depending on their or their partner's national insurance contribution record. They may also be entitled to a Christmas bonus and a winter fuel payment, which is a one-off annual payment intended to help with fuel costs.

People aged 60 and over may be entitled to receive pension credit, a means-tested benefit for people on low incomes which tops up their income to a guaranteed level and is not dependent on national insurance contributions.

Arrangements for claiming and paying pension credit are run by The Pension Service. The Pension Service does not have its own offices for people to visit, but you can contact them by telephone, through their locally based services, or through other organisations such as your local DWP office. The national telephone helpline for The Pension Service is 0800 99 1234. The Textphone number is 0800 169 0133. In Northern Ireland, The Pension Service enquiry line is 0808 601 8821. Calls are charged at local rates, and lines open 8am-8pm Monday-Saturday. The Pension Service has a website at www.thepensionservice.gov.uk, and in Northern Ireland the website address for the Social Security Agency is www.dsdni.gov.uk.

Identification and fraud

To make any benefit claim, the applicant will need to show some identification (ID). Usually they will be asked to show at least two of the following:

- a birth certificate

- driving licence

- passport

- national insurance or medical card

- recent gas or electricity bill.

They will also have to provide a national insurance number, or if they do not have one, apply for one, or provide information which will allow their number to be identified. They may have to show that the number belongs to them by providing evidence of their identity.

Claimants should be aware that the DWP and local authorities take a strict line on benefit fraud or dishonesty of any kind, including, for example, failure to advise them of changes in personal circumstances that may affect entitlement to benefit, or a claimant working when they said they were unemployed. The DWP employs fraud investigators who carry out checks with banks, education providers, HM Revenue and Customs and others to ensure that claims are valid and accurate.

Benefit fraud is a criminal offence. If the DWP or local authority has evidence that a claimant is committing benefit fraud, they can be prosecuted, or asked to pay a penalty as an alternative to prosecution.

Someone who is facing prosecution for benefit fraud or being asked to pay a penalty should seek legal advice or consult an experienced adviser.

Further information

Consumers' Association

Provides a range of leaflets on a range of issues, including debt, losing your home, welfare benefits and dealing with the police. They are also available online.

Tel: 0845 3000 343

Website:www.legalservices.gov.uk

National Debtline

Offers help and advice for anyone in debt.

Tel: 0808 808 4000

Shelterline

Provides advice and information for anyone with a housing problem.

Tel: 0808 800 4444

Welfare rights information on the web

is available from:

National Association of Citizens Advice Bureaux (NACAB): www.adviceguide.org.uk

www.shelternet.org.uk www.jobcentreplus.org.uk

www.dwp.gov.uk/lifeevent/benefits